Buds of Matata in Kenya

AMONG THE JACARANDA

Braz Menezes

To Arlene + Bob with best wishes

[signature]
December 2018

Matata Books Toronto

Copyright © 2018 Braz Menezes

Published by Matata Books, Toronto
All rights reserved. No part of this book may be used or reproduced in any manner without the written permission from the copyright holder, except in the case of short quotations embodied in critical articles or reviews.

This is a work of historical fiction based on real events. Real names have been used to honour individuals who played an important role in the life of the author. The names of Elected Politicians and Government Officials have been used in their official capacity. Other characters bearing any resemblance to real persons or events are purely coincidental or have been used in a fictional sense. Names and trademarks of organizations and institutions remain the sole property of those entities.
Care has been taken to reflect language spoken at the time, and to avoid any racial or ethnic slurs or derogatory words used in colonial times.

Cover Design and art direction: Rudi Rodrigues, Avatar Inc. Toronto
Photo: Late Leonie Menezes 1967 © Braz Menezes
Book design & layout: Rudi Rodrigues, Avatar Inc. Toronto
Editor: Reva Leah Stern, reva@revaleahstern.com

USA (CreateSpace-Assigned)
ISBN-13: 978-1724274847
ISBN-10: 1724274848

CANADA
ISBN 978-0-9877963-7-0 Paperback
ISBN 978-0-9877963-8-7 Electronic book

Library and Archives Canada Cataloguing in Publication
(to be registered after publication)
Menezes, Braz
Among The Jacaranda – Buds of Matata in Kenya

Matata Books. Canada
Contact: matatabooks@gmail.com
Website: matatabooks.com

Contents

1	My Alice in Wonderland Beginnings	1
2	Fate Disrupted	6
3	London to Liverpool	19
4	Strange and Lovely Encounters	28
5	A Cuppa	32
6	Yuletide in the UK	37
7	Assassination in Kenya	46
8	A Year of Discovery	51
9	A Stronger Cuppa	63
10	Love Isn't Necessarily Black and White	70
11	Safari to Istanbul	84
12	A Short Trip…but a Long Journey	98
13	An Arranged Marriage	109

14	Kenya, Here We Come	117
15	Eleanor's New World	130
16	Wild Animals, Tame Family	137
17	Neighbours in Our Habitat	145
18	The Highs and Lows of Life	161
19	Anxiety Becomes the Norm	170
20	Patience Is Indeed a Virtue	182
21	Working Wanderlust	195
22	Our Wheels of Fortune	205
23	The Birth of a New Day	213
24	Getting Down to Business	221
25	Preparing for Christmas	231
26	Christmas Day	245

Dedication

For Our Grandchildren
Noah, Catiyana, Isabel, Owen, Theo, Shola
And our daughters
Emily Alice, Sasha Magdalene, Catherine Silole

In Memory of

Eileen Leonie Menezes
Born Wolverhampton UK
December 1943
Died Burlington, Ontario, CANADA
July 25 2015

and
Great Grandmother

Angela Alice Costa Sa e Menezes
Born Loutolim, Salcete, GOA
April 07 1917
Died Nairobi, KENYA
December 26 1967

1

My Alice in Wonderland Beginnings

Nairobi, October 29, 1967.
The baby's estimated arrival date has passed.
"I'm sure it will be a boy!"
"Everything points to a girl!"
"It will be a big baby!"
"Definitely a small baby!"
"It will be late!"
"No doubt, it will be early!"

The multitudes of predictions by our Goan and non-Goan friends alike, in the final two weeks of Eleanor's pregnancy, are contradictory at best. The most accurate forecast could possibly be from my friend Braz Rodrigues, a virtuoso cello player at the Conservatoire of Music, an engineer and colleague… and amateur clairvoyant.

"If you would both agree to come over for a bowl of Jeanette's hot and sour soup, I can promise, the baby will arrive tonight!" So declared my friend who is on the other end of the phone which is snuggly cradled between my ear and my wife's. Braz's French wife Jeanette is a fine cook and Eleanor's eyes are signaling that we should accept the invitation.

I watch, as Eleanor gets ready for our dinner out. Her enormous Marimeko-clad belly seems to dwarf the room of our tiny two-bedroom house.

Much to my family's chagrin, we are rather sparse and unorthodox in our choice of furniture. Our bedroom has our now legendary bed and chest of drawers, and a clothes-horse by the closet. The dining room has six mahogany chairs upholstered in camel leather. Each chair back has a carved wooden shield engraved with the previous owner's family monogram. The Indian hand-craftsmanship is exquisite. The labels on the underside of the seats confirm their pedigree from McRae's, one of Nairobi's best-known wood furniture shops, catering to the wealthier class. The matching circular mahogany dining table with light-wood inlays was bought at the same time at *Muter and Oswald* auction house.

A deep red, purple and magenta rug radiates warmth and provides elegance. It was bought directly from an Arab dhow in the Old Port Mombasa for a princely sum in Kenya shillings, equivalent to about ten British pounds. We also purchased a traditional wing chair upholstered in a coarsely textured imported fabric. Instead of a sofa, we have the rear bench from our recently acquired Kombi van. A large earthen pot filled with freshly harvested papyrus fronds plucked from the stream at the bottom of the garden, sits nobly to one side of the bench. I have strung some lights to give the room a contemporary '*Habitat*' look. The Marimeko cotton fabric purchased from that chic London furnishing store was intended for drapes, but when Eleanor could not find suitable fabric or a design she liked in the Indian Bazaar, the drapery material was quickly fashioned into two very attractive maternity dresses, by my mum.

The newly decorated baby's room has a cot, a nappy-changing table and a chair and is painted in porcelain white making it quickly adaptable for a girl or boy.

We step outside onto a carpet of Jacaranda petals to say goodbye to Cloto, our Rhodesian ridgeback, and drive away to our dinner date on a street behind the Fairview Hotel on the Hill.

After a scrumptious dinner that includes an overly generous portion of hot and sour soup, we leave our hosts apartment and are barely out of the gate when Eleanor signals that her contractions have begun.

What to do? Eleanor has had her kit-bag of basics ready in the boot for the past fortnight. Last week we drove into town certain, for the second time, the baby was ready to pop out, but by the time we were at the Museum Hill roundabout by the Casino, Eleanor realized it was another false alarm and we returned home.

So, should I turn the car around and head up to the Princess Margaret Hospital, or drive home via a long, winding, badly lit and notorious road and wait at home until we're absolutely sure this time?

"I'm sorry Lando darling... I'm just a bit nervous after

hearing from your mum about the night you were born. She said, it was a short distance from Plums Lane past the Goan Gymkhana to the Lady Grigg Indian Maternity Home in Ngara, but she had to be driven there, lying on the cold steel floor, in the back of Mrs. Singh's delivery van while someone went to grab up your dad from his card game at the club. She said I should not underestimate how fast babies can make their entrance, when they've had enough of the view from inside."

I reach out and squeeze her hand. My instinct or maybe my anxiety tells me, today may be her day. "You know what, luv? Let's go to the maternity hospital just in case."

The Admission procedures at the reception desk take about twenty minutes. "I'm not expecting you to come in. I'll be fine," Eleanor says. "I'm sorry darling but we both know it could be another false alarm." I squeeze her hand and kiss her cheek to reassure her I'm okay whatever happens.

An Indian nurse escorts Eleanor into the labour room. About twenty minutes later, an African nurse walks toward me. "We think it may be a false alarm, Mr. Menezes, but we're waiting for the Chief Midwife to make the final decision.

Twenty-five minutes later the English midwife appears to deliver her verdict. "Mrs. Menezes is almost asleep, which is good for her, so we'll keep her here till the morning. I understand you have a long way to go and your wife has asked me to persuade you to go home. So, please do so and call us in the morning. I don't expect anything will happen tonight but I'll be on duty through to the 9:00 A.M. shift and to be honest, I could do with a quiet night myself. You go get some rest. Parents never have a proper night's sleep after their first born arrives."

* *

As I make my way through the whispering echoes of the hospital corridors, past echoes fill my head with the memories of an already adventurous life story. I smile and pick up the pace as I race through my journey from student en route to university in the UK to husband and soon-to-be father.

2

Fate Disrupted

Nairobi, Parklands, August, 1964

I'm packing to fly to Britain tonight. This morning I woke up to the customary chorus of birds chirping outside my window in discord with the yelping of mbwa kalis (savage dogs.) That is their usual morning address to the African laborers on their way to work.

Today, Whiskey, our Scotch terrier, is having one of his unusual but incessant barking fits. The phone rings and the barking stops abruptly, as if Whiskey is about to eavesdrop on my call.

"Hello Lando, old chap, it's me, Basil."

Basil is a secret double agent who worked for the British during the Mau-Mau uprising.

"Basil! What a surprise. To what do I owe this pleasure?"

"I heard you're leaving for the UK today. Tell me, what time will you be taking off?"

"I leave here in three hours."

"For good?" he asks. I sense urgency in his voice.

"You know I'll never leave Kenya for good, Basil. But I've

won a scholarship that's very generous when converted into Kenya shillings. It even includes beer money."

"Good for you old chap. Will you be seeing Saboti in London?" he asks.

The question strikes at my heart, which I know was not Basil's intent. "No, no! No plans on that front, Basil." Now my mind is flooded with memories of the beautiful mixed race girl, Saboti, who had once stolen my soul, then offered her heart to another. Basil and his African wife, Maua were not her parents but they had pretty much raised her.

"Er… uh, Maua sends love and best wishes too," he adds, as if to soften the faux pas he'd just committed.

"Thank you, Basil. Please give my love to Maua… I will see you both in twenty-four months. Keep well and…"

"…Lando, wait. We could also be gone by then. Lately events here have been most disturbing." His loud brash voice has shifted to a whisper.

"What do you mean?"

"About two weeks ago, two African government officials came by. They said, without explanation, that my contract had been terminated and another individual had been appointed in my place. They claimed that the order came from the highest source, which can only mean *Mzee*, President Jomo Kenyatta."

I'm searching for something comforting to say as Basil continues: "Lando, Maua is very nervous. She thinks we should take the children and head back to the UK immediately, and I can't help but feel she's right. We know too much about the dirty dealings that've been taking place with the sale and reallocation of the White-owned farms. Listen here old boy, can I ask you please to post an envelope for me in the UK? "

"Of course Basil, but how will I get it?"

"My friend Stewart Wallace will meet you at the airport and hand it to you; I would be most grateful. Now, please forget everything I've told you about the goings on in the past here. It must remain between us. So, mum's the word, alright?"

"Sure, but Basil…!" I hear a click as Basil abruptly hangs up.

I step out into the garden to settle my thoughts. Whiskey is laying on his side growling and pawing furiously at an intimate itch. I leave him to it and return to my room. I'm quite unnerved by Basil's news. It's not like him to overreact. I glance at my watch, place one knee on my bloated leather suitcase and lock it up.

I've lived at my parent's house on Plums Lane since birth, but for the past five years I've been a tenant in their converted garage. It's my own private space where I can freely admire the grotesque yet sensuous clay models from my architectural training days, as well as the gently-moving sculpture I've created from bicycle and wooden model parts, and other odds and ends, as in a half-finished Alexander Calder mobile.

I sit pensively on my bed and muse at how the sun's rays cast a warm glow over my red and purple sisal rug. Suddenly my reverie is interrupted.

"Lando, Lando, come quickly." Niven, my little thirteen

year old brother pokes his head inside.

"You remember Toto who was killed during the Mau-Mau?"

"Toto? You mean Stephen?"

"Yes, Toto, Stephen whatever... well, he's here."

"Niven, if he was killed, how can he be here?"

"I don't know. Dad sent me to call you to come quickly." With that, Niven jumps over the patch of geraniums by my front door and sprints back to the main house. I'm confused, but if my father calls, I must go.

Of course I remember Stephen. A mischievous seven-year-old, always ready to run any errand for me, as long as I'd let him polish my new bicycle. He always dreamed he would one day own one like it.

His family were of the Kikuyu tribe who were both hated and feared by the colonial government. Stephen's father, Mwangi, worked for us and lived in our servants' quarters. In 1952 he had fled his village and brought his pregnant wife Wangari and their two year old son Stephen to live with him. The Mau-Mau would kill or maim the families of male adults who did not take the Mau-Mau oath.

In 1954, armed *askaris* (policemen) searching for Mau-Mau suspects in Nairobi raided our home and took Stephen's family away. We never had contact with any of them again. We heard that the men were taken to remote detention camps where they were tortured and 'exorcised' of their oath. The women and children were resettled in 'village camps.' Their family land was confiscated and redistributed to those

Kikuyus loyal to the government. So, how was it possible he could return after ten years? Niven must have misunderstood.

I step out and shut my door. Although it's sunny overhead, to the southwest, dark clouds are gathering. As I enter the main house, the smell of fresh baking drifts from Mum's kitchen.

A man is sitting on a straight-back chair looking somewhat nervous. He stands up to greet me. I struggle with my words until finally I hear myself say:

"Stephen, it's truly you. *Karibu* (welcome)." I'm stunned. "You are no longer *mtoto*! (A little boy). You are now *kijana* (A young man)." I speak to him in Swahili.

Stephen holds out his right hand in greeting, with his head slightly bowed as a sign of respect. His eyes are moist.

"*Bwana* Lando, I am so very happy to see you again," he replies in English.

"It really is you, Stephen!" I take and hold his outstretched hand. I feel a lump in my throat and tears well up in my eyes. My Dad wipes at his own moist lids.

"Please sit down and tell us where you've been. What news of Mwangi and Wangari and your little sister, Mary?" my father urges.

Mum suddenly jumps up and pleads. "Wait, please don't talk until I return with the tea tray." Dad gestures for her to sit-down, but she rushes from the room, no doubt hiding her own tears.

My mother had told me several years ago that the armed *askaris* arrived at our home one morning in 1954. They were rounding up innocent people at gunpoint and taking them away. A European officer shouted orders to his men: "You there, search behind the building. You two, search every inch of these quarters. These animals will not escape."

Stephen seems fidgety and nervous. I want to ask him so many questions. Where has he been all this time? Where was his family? Are they alive and safe? But I hesitate to ask. For now, I will listen to what he's prepared to tell.

This re-emerging friendly ghost appears to be sleep-deprived. His lids slowly lower for an instant, but when they reopen, his eyes seem vacant.

Anja returns with a pot of tea and a home-baked cake. She places a large slice in front of Stephen who delights in the treat and is clearly overjoyed to have found me and the rest of his 'Goan family' again. It had taken him time to piece together directions to Plums Lane, which he once knew so well as a child.

"So now Stephen, tell us where you've been for ten years, and how you got back here, and news of your family," my mother urges. Obviously, she doesn't share my hesitation.

He ponders for a moment and then between bites of cake, he begins to weave together the pieces of his memory. He remembers the police kicking in the door of the servants' quarters and shouting instructions in Swahili and English. He remembers running out and grabbing onto my mother's dress and peeking out from behind her and watching as his father, Mwangi, is dragged out of their home and brutally prodded with their rifles. When he saw his mother emerge, holding his baby sister, he let go of my Mum's dress and rushed screaming to his mother's side.

They all saw his father being brutally struck again and again with rifle butts as they forced him onto a lorry that was already loaded with suspects. Eventually, but separately, Stephen, his mother and baby sister were also taken away.

As Stephen continues to talk, I study the features of this seventeen-year-old man who is eight years younger and now three inches taller than me. But no doubt, shaped by his years in a detention camp, he has a strong frame and a muscular body. Still evident, on his left cheek, is the now less-pronounced scar that he incurred when he took my new bicycle for a spin and landed his seven-year-old self in a thorny kai-apple hedge.

"I did not see my father again. He did not see his children again. The government killed him ten years ago." He speaks in short clipped sentences as he tries to remember facts… or maybe omit disturbing details.

He takes a deep replenishing breath and turns to face me. "Do you have work for me Bwana Lando? I must earn money for my mother and sister. We have nothing now."

I'm taken aback. "Then what have you been doing until now to earn money, Stephen?"

He explains that he has been working as a tout for *matatus* (minivans), transporting passengers daily between the city and African town ships and squatter camps on the periphery of Nairobi.

"Are *matatus* not illegal?" my father asks.

"Illegal? Yes, but poor Africans have no other means of transport, Bwana Daddy. People are packed in like goats. It is very dangerous work. There are many young people ready to do terrible things to take my job. To get a good job you must know important people. This is why I come to *Bwana* Lando."

"Stephen, I'm leaving for England tonight… in about two hours."

He seems panicked on hearing my news.

"You don't mean you are going to live there, forever?" he anxiously asks.

"No. I'm only going for two years for further studies. I will be back. I'm so sorry, I can't help you with a job."

I feel dreadful, even guilty. I look toward Dad for inspiration but he too is at a loss.

Suddenly I blurt out a suggestion. "Stephen, you must look for work while I'm away. However, I will make arrangements for you to receive a bit of money each month to help out. I will get it to Bwana Daddy and you will come and get it from him each month. But I warn you, it won't be enough. You will still need to work."

I excuse myself and go to my room. I return with ten notes, in ten-shilling denominations. I hand them to Stephen who gratefully and quickly stows them in his pocket.

"Thank you. Thank you, Bwana Lando." He stands up to leave. "I must to go now before it is night. We have many *wakora* (robbers) these days."

He shakes Chico's hand, kisses Anja's hand, and bows slightly. He holds both my hands and I embrace him.

"Bwana Lando, maybe you will meet Her Majesty the Queen. She will not be coming back again to Kenya, I think."

"Wait, Stephen." Anja shouts as she approaches him with a small package. "Please take this to Wangari… and there is also something in there for Mary," she says, "And give me another minute to wrap up some cake for you."

Moments later, with treasured packages in hand, Stephen walks briskly down the drive towards Plums Lane, turning back just once to wave. The family stands watching in silent wonder.

Anja interrupts the mood. "Lando, you had better finish off your packing, Ahmad will be here in about an hour and you must eat something."

"Thanks Mum but they will feed us on the plane… and I'm packed."

* *

We are all in Ahmad's black Chevy heading for the recently built Jomo Kenyatta International Airport at Embakasi on the edge of the Athi Plains. The sky is almost black and the air is heavy. I look back and notice that Mum has snuggled closer to Dad.

Barely a mile from the airport, hailstones begin to lash at the windshield. Now for certain, Mum will see the dark clouds as a bad luck omen.

My mother whispers to my father amid the clattering hail.

"Chico, did you have a chance to talk to him about it?"

"About what, *Amorsinha?*"

"About concentrating on his studies and bringing back a

diploma."

"I'm sure he will do that..." Dad says with a reassuring smile.

"Chico, you spend too much time playing cards with your friends and ignoring what's happening in the world outside. Our Goan boys are leaving their diplomas behind in England and returning with *Mzungu* (white) wives."

"*Amorsinha*, last time, I spoke to Lando about Saboti, correct? And did he listen to my advice? No! And we still don't know what really happened between them. England is a small place. Don't be surprised if they meet up and start all that *matata* (trouble) over again."

Anja sits back in her seat, eyes welling with tears.

I look toward Ahmad, his hands firmly gripping the wheel. He flashes me a judgmental raised eyebrow, as only he can. He has been with our family for most of my life. He left Karachi as a highly qualified engineer. He worked with the Railways for one contract, but left disgusted at the discrimination on pay scales between whites and non-whites. My father helped him purchase a taxi. The result is that Ahmad has remained a friend who considers himself family, and moreover a *therapist* to anyone who seeks his advice.

He pulls into the airport where a few close friends are waiting to see me off. Soon after, Mum and Dad say their heartfelt farewells. Ahmad pulls me aside and whispers. "Please listen to me, Lando, don't disappear in England forever, or you will break your mother's heart."

"Never!" I reassure him with a grin.

I am somewhat apprehensive travelling to the UK. According to newspaper reports, there has been a constant stream of coloured immigration into Britain, and a consequent sharp rise in anti-immigrant protests and blunt racism.

In the airport lounge, I exchange last goodbyes with my friends and proceed toward the immigration line.

I stop abruptly when I hear my name being shouted in a whisper. "Lando, psst, Lando?" I turn and encounter a well-dressed European man looking me over.

"Yes, I'm Lando but…"

"… Good. Basil asked me to meet you here."

"Oh, yes, of course. You're Stewart Wallace." I blush slightly as I realize that in my preoccupation with my bon voyage well-wishers, I had completely forgotten about Basil's call. While I extend my hand in greeting, Stewart Wallace withdraws a thick sealed envelope from a worn leather bag, plants it in my outstretched hand, and disappears into the crowd.

I shrug, place the envelope in my backpack and join the line-up.

I'm proud to see my young fellow Kenyans, dressed in their smart, well pressed uniforms and carrying out their tasks efficiently. Their job is to check for the dreaded tax-clearance certificate, the amount of currency on my person, unlawful archaeological souvenirs, unlicensed gemstones, and other export-restricted items. I'm grateful that everything moves smoothly and courteously, contrary to the predictions of many non-Africans who are certain that: 'standards would drop after independence.'

The passengers commence the walk across the tarmac to the plane. On board, I make my way to my seat where the jostle for space in the luggage-bins is in full swing. The crowd of Asian families with British passports who are leaving Kenya permanently seem to have been allowed extra carry-ons. Last minute purchases of sheepskin jackets, duty-free booze, Mkamba woodcarvings and Kisi soapstone sculptures are being forced into the tight bins that appear to expand to oblige.

The flight is ready for take-off. I lean back in my seat. My thoughts turn to Stephen and his desperate situation. I am comforted somewhat by the fact that I left thirty signed checks for him, with my Dad.

**

Three years prior to graduation from Architectural school, I had filled out numerous application forms and attached countless letters, essays, and references. I had applied for bursaries and scholarships to go abroad for continuing study, but priority was clearly given to well-connected African students. I used to believe that, being brown, I led a less privileged life than the *Wazungu* (white people). But it seems if you are born black here, and have no connection to the black political elite, you have no privilege at all. Thankfully, I was awarded a Royal British Commonwealth Scholarship to study urban planning in Liverpool.

I leaf through the information folder I received from the British Council Office in Nairobi and open up the British

Railways map. I can't help but contrast the complicated spider's web of rail lines crisscrossing England, to the solitary rail line that connects Mombasa on the Indian Ocean with Kampala in Uganda. As I study all the main rail destinations out of London, so many familiar cities come rushing back to me from my high school history lessons.

I find myself distracted. My two white seat-mates, who were already-piss-drunk and overtly amorous when they boarded, have continued to drink and make out with abandon. I can't help but wonder if they will try to copulate next to me? I notice that I'm not the only "spy" on board. As the flight attendant places a much welcomed whiskey and soda in my hand, I can see that she is also keeping a very watchful eye on the inebriated and animated couple.

Back to the map. It strikes me as kind of ironic that in high school, I wrote an exam on the impact of the colonies, the industrial revolution in England, and the growth of the British Commonwealth; and now I'm travelling on a British Commonwealth Scholarship.

The amorous couple seem to have finally succumbed to sleep.

Now my worries turn to whether my sister, Linda, received my telegram and will meet me at Heathrow Airport. But perhaps I should set my concern aside because there are always taxicabs and I'm pretty sure I now have the British rail system worked out.

I drift off to a restless sleep.

3

London to Liverpool

A beautiful morning welcomes us as the VC10 makes a smooth landing at Heathrow. The passengers disembark and walk an interminable distance along nondescript corridors to an immigration hall packed with hordes of sleep-deprived passengers from across the globe. Distraught immigration attendants direct exhausted new-arrivals into queues. Anxious heads of households nervously clutch vital documents. I step forward imagining the worst-case scenario. What if I'm missing some crucial paper? Will they pack me off on the same plane back to Nairobi that evening?

Clutching my Kenyan Passport and my student visa, I step in front of an officer who barely glances at my passport, or me, but carefully studies my visa.

"What will you be studying?" he asks without modulating his voice or raising his head.

"Town planning. The program is called Civic Design, at the University of Liverpool." He presses his glasses against the bridge of his nose and looks through me.

"Will you stay on in the United Kingdom after your graduation?" The officer's thick black frames make his icy blue eyes appear terrifyingly unfriendly.

"No sir," I reply. "I have a job waiting when I get home."

"Aha. Okay then. Welcome to the country and good luck." The officer smiles, stamps both documents and hands them to me. "Next."

Outside the customs hall, amid waving hands and bobbing signboards, I spot Linda. She has shed her winter attire and opted for more tropical plumage. By her side is her English husband, David, dressed as a proper Brit in grey slacks and a sober plaid shirt.

"What took you so long?" she jokes. "There are a zillion people here. Your plane must have been stacking passengers in the baggage compartment."

I have missed my sister's quick wit. "I know, I think all the civil servants, from British East Africa decided to come to England, on my plane."

"They're coming from the ex-colonies" David says, "East Africa, the Caribbean, India, Egypt, Hong Kong and everywhere else."

Linda interjects. "Oh, by the way, I met some of your ex-Royal Tech buddies at a party at East Africa House. They said I have to bring you around some time.

"Listen Lando, I didn't want to stir up sad memories of Saboti, and your last trip, so we'll take a different route home this time."

I convince myself that I've firmly locked out 'the Saboti affair' as I now call it. It's terminated. Kaput! So I respond. "Fine by me."

As we drive along, I can't help but recall my first visit to London. I was on a mission to find Saboti, my true love. I remember the anguish in her eyes when she realized how much I cared, but had to tell me, it was over. If only she had waited, had faith, and hadn't panicked. In the days following my return to Kenya, I struggled to pick up the fragments of my broken heart, which was as hopeless as picking up the splintered remains of a shattered windscreen from a gravel road.

"We're home," David says. He eases the car to the curb and lets us out with the luggage before going to park.

* *

Over breakfast, Linda and David discuss sightseeing plans for the next few days. My mind is anywhere but there.

"Hey, earth to Lando. We want our funny Lando back!" Linda insists. "Listen, a *first love* happens to everyone. It's called puppy love, so get over it."

"It's okay for you to talk, you have your love right there," I mumble.

My sister will not let up. "Lando, you have a great opportunity to expand your world. Please, just get on with your life."

Eight years in London has toughened her. "Listen, Lando, imagine being in Dad's shoes when he was orphaned in his early teens. He sailed from India to Africa in the mid-twenties with no idea where he'd land, what he'd find there, or who he'd meet. He just knew he'd have to make a life for himself and he never looked back."

That night I reflect on our conversation and vow I will

indeed try my best to start again and live my life to the fullest.

Three days later, I'm bound for Liverpool. I'm standing at London's Euston Station, which is in utter disarray. A notice explains it's undergoing a major renovation to prepare for the electrification of the North-Western rail system. I make my way to Platform 9.

* *

The train pulls into Liverpool's Lime Street Station, the home of the Beatles who just five months earlier had completed a first tour of the USA and had become an instant global success.

I wait as other passengers jostle about, grab their suitcases, and scurry off the train. I stand up to help my elderly seatmate with her bag, then we wait together for the crowd to thin out before we exit.

There is a general belief that the English are cold and private, but when she chose the seat beside me at Euston, I introduced myself as being newly arrived in England, and from that moment on, the lady confided in me, as if I were her parish priest. She explained that she was returning from a visit with her only surviving cousin who has advanced lung cancer and was given just six months to live. She loathed the British National Health Service, and seemed to have given up on politicians of every stripe. "They're thieves who only want power and your money," she insisted.

I tell her I'm amazed by what she said. "Frankly, Ma'am, anyone daring to call Europeans, 'thieves' in Kenya would bring serious *matata*, sorry, trouble on themselves."

The lady continues. "Kenya? Isn't that where those dreadful Mau-Mau are slaughtering white people by the thousands?"

"Not anymore," I say. "In fact, they've killed thousands more of their own kind than they have Europeans. On December 12th of last year, Kenya became an independent nation and is no longer your, uh… a colony of Britain."

"Good," she says. "I don't believe in having overseas colonies just so our upper crust can have copious numbers of servants at their beck and call."

"That era is over," I confirm.

"Do you know a Vishnoo Patel?" she asks. "He's from Kenya. He's owns our local grocer shop and has been doing miracles with it. He, or one of his sons, will deliver our groceries right to our door. Imagine that! I hope we have many more Vishnoos. It will change Britain for the better."

I am surprised by her comment. Perhaps she missed the bold headlines at the newsstand that were screaming out for immediate curbs on unlimited coloured immigration into Britain.

"Well young man, we're here. It's been a pleasure talking with you. I'm sure you will be very successful in your studies. And you will love our Liverpudlians. You'll likely find that they speak rather funny, but from the heart."

We shake hands, she takes her bag and scurries along.

I stand on the platform, mesmerized by the roof over the station train shed, a magnificent half-round cylinder constructed in iron and glass that covers a number of tracks. It might have been built in the mid-nineteenth century when the British Empire under Queen Victoria was at its industrial peak.

I pick up my case and walk under the arched entryway and exit to the taxi line. Before I get into the cab, I hand the driver a paper with the address of the International Students Hostel. He babbles a response in a strange tongue and I'm beginning to panic. The lady had warned me that they spoke funny, but this is a completely foreign language. As the driver has already dumped my case into the cab, I have no alternative but to get in.

He lets me off in front of a brick building on Mount Pleasant bearing the sign, 'The International Students Hostel.' I'm relieved to have arrived at the correct address... and safely.

As I enter, Mrs. Robinson, a well-coiffed, grey-haired warden cynically asks, "Shall I presume the train was late?"

"I'm so sorry to have inconvenienced you, Mrs. Robinson. They delayed the departure time out of London without warning," I stammer.

She peers into a registration book. I notice the crow's feet under her pink framed glasses. She has a kind face but with the same penetrating blue eyes of the immigration officer. On the back wall of the small reception cubicle, I see a bank of pigeonholes, with name plates above each section.

"Mr. Menezes, The British Council provided us with all the information we need for your registration. There are just a few papers to sign; then once you have established a bank account, we can process a standing order for your weekly rent and board." She hands me a package that includes the 'Hostel Rules' and floor plans of the different levels. "Mr. Menezes, in case of fire, please acquaint yourself with the emergency exits."

"Please call me Lando, Ma'am."

She glances at my room number, unhooks a key from one of the boards and hands it to me. "Well, Lando, you are in one of our most interesting attic rooms," she says. "It's on the third floor. So, in case of fire, it may be easier to climb out the window... slide down the roof, and pray a fireman will catch you in time."

I wince at the thought, and hope she's joking. She smiles and winks.

"Off you go now and get some rest. Dinner will be in the dining room at 6:30 P.M. sharp. If you miss it, like other boarders, you might have to try foraging for food in the neighbourhood. So I would not recommend you get into a habit of being late."

I grab my suitcase, which for some reason, seems heavier now than at the start of my journey. I struggle with it down the narrow corridor and up the stairs to the first floor. I pause to catch my breath before heading up a second flight of stairs.

A six-foot, broad-shouldered giant suddenly opens a door. I squeeze into a niche near a removable fire extinguisher which I consider will be handy, in case I need a weapon. The man looks at me quizzically. "Hello. Okay not mind. Sorry my *Ingleesh*, not good. You new here now? Okay?"

"Yes, new. I'm Orlando from Kenya. You can call me

Lando."

"Me also new. One week before. My name, Giovanni Abrantes Santos Goveia from Rio de Janeiro, Brazil. But you must to call me Nelson." He extends his large meaty hand as I offer my small limp paw in return. His firm, strong grip makes me wonder if any of my bones survived intact after his eager handshake.

"Where is room? I help you."

Nelson picks up the case as if it were a loaf of bread and races up the next two flights. He sets it down outside of room 3B. He offers another handshake but spares me the full impact this time.

"Maybe we eat together for dinner, yes? But also I may be not here." And with that confusing message he leaves as quickly as he arrived.

I glance around the tiny room that is to be my home for the next two years. It didn't require my architect-trained eyes to notice the exposed electric conduits that were lavishly coated with glossy green paint. There is a high sloping ceiling, a single bed, a four drawer dresser, and an alcove for hanging suits. A small desk and chair are tucked under the narrow window, and next to it, a coin-operated gas fire. The very idea of this dangerous device sends a shiver up my spine. I'm relieved that winter is still a few months away.

I unpack everything and am delighted to find that the suitcase fits snuggly under the desk.

I pick up a towel and head for the community bathroom at the end of the passageway. It's a cramped space. The water is barely tepid. Several people in Kenya had warned me of the relative frugality of life in ordinary British homes compared to that of their white compatriots in the colonies. Now I'm a believer.

Back in my room, I peer through the window and catch a glimpse of the sloping slate roof under my windowsill. Maybe Mrs. Robinson wasn't kidding about the fire escape.

I spread out the Liverpool City Map on the desk to get my bearings. I can see that the hostel is a short walk from the University. Since much of the staff at the University in Nairobi, was recruited from Liverpool, I had heard a lot about their architectural heritage and city planning, so it was all beginning to feel familiar.

In spite of the sparse living conditions and the Brazilian giant residing downstairs, I'm feeling safe in Liverpool. I sit on the edge of the bed and look over the information pamphlet Mrs. Robinson gave me. My eyelids seem to be involuntarily closing. I spread out on the bed for a quick nap.

It's 9:30 P.M. and I've missed dinner and the evening news. After being nurtured on the World Service my entire life, I was looking forward to hearing the BBC direct from London.

"If you rush now, you may catch the fish and chip place before it closes," a fellow resident informs me.

As I hurry to leave for the fish and chip shop, I spot the envelope I was handed at the Kenya airport and notice something odd. The stamp, mailing address and return address are all United Kingdom. I drop it into the post box as promised.

4

Strange and Lovely Encounters

September, 1964

Two days later, I meet up again with Nelson.

"Your name, Lando. Brazilian, yes? Why, then you don't speak Portuguese?"

I tell him about my father's travels from Goa to Africa looking for work, and about my would-have-been-priest uncle, who escaped from Rachol Seminary in Goa then died in Angola, en route to Brazil."

"Oh," Nelson says. "Mine uncle, Urico Goveia, killed in Angola, 1949. He on safari. His family never go again to Africa."

"I was born in Kenya and I will never leave Africa," I tell him. We talk instead, about Brazilian soccer star Pele and the forthcoming 1966 World Cup matches to be played in England.

Nelson says he is studying English, and event and project management, for two years. He will then return to Brazil after the games because his real love is soccer and organizing big events with local musicians. He offers to guide me around the best music clubs in Liverpool.

"That will be fun." I say. "*Obrigado*."

* *

It's late in September, and the weather has turned decidedly crisp with a chill Atlantic wind blowing from the Docks. The sun has made an appearance after two consecutive days of rain. Fallen autumn leaves have glued themselves to the pavement. The short walk up Mount Pleasant to Abercrombie Square offers new sensory experiences of light, sound and smell that are very distinct from those in Nairobi. I miss the clear blue skies and unfiltered sunshine; the tweets and chirping of birds; the smell of wet earth after the rain. This distinct separation of seasons is a big change for me.

Stores have begun marketing woollies and thermal underwear and something I had never heard of... *electric* blankets. I stand outside a shop window and gawk, trying to figure out how this works. I try to imagine myself snuggling up under an electric blanket, but in my mind, the blanket suddenly shorts out and bursts into flame. I imagine Mrs. Robinson discovering my charred remains the next day and wondering why I didn't simply open the window and slide down the roof.

The School of Planning and Civic Design is a modern grey steel and brick building set in one corner of a very attractive Georgian Square. Inside, our course work has begun in earnest. Our student group is best described as an assorted bag of 'fruits and nuts.' Women outnumber men, about sixty percent to forty. Another twenty percent of the total are mature-age post-graduate foreigners who are accompanied by their wives.

They come from Jordan, Nigeria, Bangladesh and Columbia. In their countries of origin, they held important positions and titles, and now seem to resent their status as mere students. In spite of it, they all appear to have somehow adjusted to life in Liverpool.

The social life for students is hectic. My male colleagues and I routinely visit jazz spots, dance clubs and popular pubs. One of the best, and my favourite, is Liverpool's famous Philharmonic Pub with its beautifully carved mahogany interior embellished with marble, stained glass, and intricate plasterwork that would make the Taj Mahal proud. Even the gentlemen's toilet is encrusted with mosaic, quartz and marble tiles and endowed with a treasured urinal to pee in and a precious throne on which to set a warm bottom.

Since Nelson and I were both keen to visit the Cavern Club on Mathew Street where the Beatles music was born, my giant Brazilian friend insisted we try to get in. We arrive one Friday night, to find an enormous queue at the door.

"Lando, you stay here now," Nelson says.

Within minutes, he's back. "Come. We have ticket. But you must to speak only Portuguese until we go in. I tell doorman, we come special from Brazil to see the Bethlehem of Beatles and we must to return next day." He winks. "We Brazilians have a *jeitino* (way of doing things) yes?"

The giant smoke-filled cellar is packed with young people who have no concerns but to enjoy the music and the moment. They chat noisily cloistered inside the smoke-filled, brick-arched alcoves and short tunnels that lead off the main area.

"Hey Lando," a female voice calls out. "Over here."

Nelson and I make our way toward the voice, which I discover is coming from a classmate.

"Hey, hi Jenny, I didn't expect to find you here."

"I love this place" Jenny replies. "You can find us here every weekend. This is my friend Margaret from the History Department."

"Hi. And this is my friend Nelson from Brazil. What do you think the chances are the Beatles will stop by to play for us tonight?" I offer with a wink.

"Ha, ha! We'll have to be happy with their ghosts," Margaret says. "Last time they played here was a year ago, August. By the way, if you're a fan, next Saturday, there will be a big auction of Beatle wood."

"What's that?" I query.

Margaret explains "Their old stage is being removed and the wood will be cut up into tiny pieces like chocolate bars and sold as Beatle souvenirs."

"I hear the Americans are lining up to buy it all." Jenny smirks. "I would too, if it was actually chocolate."

"*Americanos*, buy everything," Nelson adds, and then without explanation, he walks away.

When the evening is done, the girls head out, and I go in search of Nelson. I find him holding forth with a bevy of gorgeous au pairs from Portugal, Spain and Sweden.

Clearly, his poor *Ingleesh* is no longer a handicap.

5

A Cuppa

Liverpool, September, 1964

I've already acquired certain idiosyncrasies from the natives, such as drinking tea at the slightest provocation. It is on such a tea-making mission to the Common Room at the University that I have my first encounter with Eleanor Pearson, a graduate with a BA in Sociology. Our paths have crossed periodically, but not our voices. I spot her, comfortably seated in a sumptuous armchair, engrossed in a book. I can't help but notice the word 'sex' in the title. I wouldn't have suspected her of being the type. That opinion is likely coloured by the fact that my English colleagues had already classified the twenty something blonde as being shy, prim and proper. The alcove, where she is seated, is an ideal location. Its large bay window frames the beauty of the autumn trees like a Great Master's oil painting.

"Hello Eleanor," I say quietly, trying not to disturb her, "I'm making myself a *cuppa*. Fancy one?"

Eleanor looks up momentarily. "No, thank you… I've drunk my rations for the day." She turns back to her book.

I give my tea a quick stir and take a seat opposite her by the same picture window that frames the city skyline panorama. The new Metropolitan Catholic Cathedral now dominates the view as it rises amidst a sea of black slate-tiled roofs and red brick Victorian town houses.

Eleanor looks up and smiles.

"Lando, you're an architect, right? So, what do you think of that design?"

"Oh, well... uh, I'd say it's not as dramatic as Oscar Niemeyer's design for the Cathedral in Brasilia which is also a conical shape and conceived at about the same time," I reply, hoping a bit of namedropping will impress her. "I'd also add that the winning design by British architect Fredrick Gibberd probably addressed the requirements best."

"What do you mean?" She closes the book and places it on her lap.

It worked. Eleanor is impressed... or at least, curious. I continue. "His design had to incorporate the original, partly-constructed crypt designed by Edwin Luytens, the architect of New Delhi, and many other architectural works in Imperial India. That condition rather forced the shape of the structure."

"I'm impressed."

Then I've succeeded... but I still continue. "Actually I was a draughtsman with a team assembled by a Nairobi architect who submitted a design for the original competition in 1960. We were competing with about 300 architects from around the world."

"That's remarkable," she generously offers. "Lando… did you ever go to school in England?"

"No, why do you ask?"

"Well, I remember visiting the Wolverhampton Town Hall with my mother. I was six years old then, and my grandfather was the Mayor. He and some Aldermen had gathered to welcome Dr. Lamba, the first Indian doctor, to their city. He became our family doctor, and I used to giggle each time the doctor turned to my granddad, bowed and said, 'Your Worship, Sir Mayor Pearson Sir, Thank you.' It was so endearing. Anyway, I ask because the doctor was accompanied by his plump 12-year-old son, who spoke posh English, like you. But then, you're much too skinny to be him."

"Thank you, I think. Tell me, Eleanor, why did you move on from Sociology to study Urban Planning?"

She smiles. "Well, I could say that a few of us decided to hang in here at University to find husbands. But the truth is, there are no interesting jobs for new graduate sociologists, and as long as we can receive student grants, it makes sense to stay on and further our studies.

"Tell me, Lando, do you find England very different from Kenya?"

"Of course. For example, in Nairobi, daylight arrives at 6:30 A.M. year-round without fail, and darkness falls like a curtain at 6:30 P.M. All my life I ate dinner after sundown, so it's unnatural for my body to feel hungry before dark. Consequently, for the first few days here, I would arrive back at the hostel starving, only to find the dining room and kitchen locked for the night."

"You have obviously survived." Eleanor smiles.

I return the smile. "Yes, in Kenya we develop food-gathering skills from birth. I've learned to hunt for food in the jungle of stores around Mt. Pleasant. I also have a small stockpile of dire emergency snacks in my room."

"When I lived in student dorms, storing food in our rooms was strictly prohibited."

"Really? Why?"

"Because of rodents," she says with a shudder.

"Rodents? You mean big rats? Or little mice?"

"I don't care. I'm terrified and sickened by the sight of either. But that's history. I'm now in digs that I share with a friend until May of next year when I plan to move into something even better."

"I guess I too will have to get out of the international hostel soon. Our prim and proper Mrs. Robinson enforces too many restrictions on our comings and goings… and 'visitors' for that matter."

"Okay, tell me, what were your first notable impressions of Liverpool?"

"Well, I was really surprised to see white men sweeping streets, collecting garbage, and driving buses. In Kenya, those jobs are only for Africans."

"Here everyone has to work," she states.

"There's another thing that's different," I admit. "In Kenya, while Africans and Asians work long hours, the European men leave work early and go to their clubs to play tennis, squash, badminton or rugby. Here in Liverpool, especially on weekends, I see coloured people playing soccer or cricket and even sunbathing in the parks, while white people work."

"It's very true. I just never thought of it," Eleanor muses.

I look at my watch and excuse myself. Eleanor picks up her book and while I strain to get a look at the cover, she senses my interest and holds it high so I can see the title. She reads it aloud. "'*The Second Sex*' by Simone de Beauvoir. You must read it, Lando. In fact, I propose that all men must read it," she jestingly instructs.

Walking home, Mum's words to Dad on the drive to the airport are echoing in my head:

'*Boys are leaving their certificates behind in England and bringing back white brides to Kenya.*' Then I recall Eleanor joking about girls hanging on at University to find husbands… at least I think she was joking. Regardless, it certainly wasn't going to happen to me. She's smart though. She had extracted a lot of information from me while I learned virtually nothing about her. No matter. I will be keeping a safe distance from her and her husband-hunting mates.

6

Yuletide in the UK

December, 1964

Christmas is almost here and the letters from Kenya are more emotional than usual. Mum writes: *all the Indian shopkeepers on Biashara Street have not yet left for Britain, as was rumoured. All the streets are packed with shoppers. Oh yes, and Stephen dropped by with a gift of a live hen. By the way, your niece, Linet, is already five months old. She's a beautiful child and Fatima says she's no trouble at all. I'm so happy. I hope they give me more grandchildren.*

Dad writes: *people of all races were happy on this first Anniversary of Uhuru (Independence) when Kenya was declared a Republic. But. Lando, it feels empty at home with you and Linda away in England, and Joachim still in America. He says Yale is very demanding and he is looking forward to returning home soon. So it will be just Frank and Niven with us this Christmas. Now, that Frank has turned three, he thinks he's a grownup and he wants to go to Yale to see Joachim.*

I write back: *Tell Frank, I wish I could be home with him and all of you, but no worries, I will be spending the holidays with*

Linda and David in London.

I know Mum will be especially pleased about that. I tell them about my discovery of electric blankets in the UK.

* *

Linda greets me at London's Euston Station effervescing with energy.

"First, we'll drop your suitcase at our place, then Dave and I want to give you a taste of your first Christmas in London."

Within minutes we are scurrying down steps onto crowded rail platforms, deep underground. A train arrives, disgorges passengers, and then sucks up the waiting throngs into its belly once again. We are squished onto a corner bench. Many stops later, Linda pulls on my arm. "Come Lando and listen to me; people won't hear that polite, 'excuse me Sir.' Here, you have to push your way through the throngs."

We exit at the South Kensington Station. I've just had my first ride in the Tube, London's famous underground system. It's a complex network of crisscrossing tunnels that reminds me of a giant worm colony.

After a quick snack, we're off again. A short double-decker bus ride away, we enter the Tube again and exit at Oxford Circus. I've never seen crowds of shoppers on this scale before. David is providing a non-stop commentary on key landmarks, explaining the orientation of main arterial streets, and occasionally admitting he's lost.

We walk down Regent Street, which is dazzlingly decorated with illuminated design motifs strung from lamppost to lamppost. Although it's late afternoon, the lights are already on. It's not difficult to imagine how fabulous it will look at nightfall.

At Harrods, the window mannequins are bedecked in their finest furs, cashmere and silk, and adorned with sparkling jewelry. They beckon us to enter the store… but we resist.

"Come, let me show you something special." Linda takes my hand. "This way."

We all turn left onto a laneway, leaving the traffic and noise of Regent Street and walk eastward a short block where we come to a sign that stops me in my tracks:

'CARNABY STREET, CITY OF WESTMINSTER'

"I'm sure you might have heard of this place, even in far-off Kenya?" Linda chuckles.

"It's only the trendiest spot in London," I confirm.

And it does not disappoint; with its elaborate window displays, quaint pubs, and bistros with their hand-crafted menus. Small storefronts are painted in bright turquoise, reds, greens and yellows with their shop names painted in contrasting colours.

People are scurrying in all directions, like they're fleeing from a disturbed anthill.

Bright overhead banners displaying huge photos of the Beatles are strung along the length of the street while Beatles music blares from PA systems hung from shop fronts and street lamps.

"You can see this area is for the younger set," David says.

"That's me," I joke.

"You're twenty-five my dear brother, and twenty-five is ancient to these teeny boppers."

I mindlessly bump into a man wearing a bright blue turban and a turquoise embroidered tunic over red stovepipe trousers. "Oops! I'm so sorry." I apologize profusely but he doesn't even give me the courtesy of accepting.

"That was rude of him," I mutter. Linda doubles over laughing and pointing.

Then I get it. The man is one of many life-like mannequins placed randomly along the street. I blush and as I look around to see who else witnessed my embarrassing moment, I spot a black man decked out in white ballooning trousers, a brightly-coloured Nigerian shirt, and a WWII German helmet; and he's shaking his head in disapproval. I'm relieved to see that he too is a mannequin.

"This area is called SoHo," David informs me with the professional cadence of a tour guide. "Let's move along now."

And so it goes. Every day and evening there's a packed agenda. Covent Garden Market; a walk along the Thames Embankment: a stop at Madame Tussaud's Wax Museum with their new Beatles exhibit; and a special visit to the Hammersmith Palais, a dance hall built like a warehouse that is about fifty times larger than our Goan Gymkhana Hall.

Linda explains that "the Palais is the place where people from small towns and cities in the UK, as well as foreigners, can come to meet someone of the opposite sex to dance with, or maybe just make some friends in this crowded and sometimes lonely city. There are events happening here every night of the week."

"This used to be a tram shed, but in the twenties it was converted into a dance hall," David explains. "My parents used to come dancing here before the War.

We join the queue and purchase our tickets.

We follow Linda, who seems to know where she's going. At the far end, to my surprise, we meet up with three old Goan friends of mine from Kenya and another friend, George, from Zanzibar. All are now living in London. It had been a few years and we had lost contact. We are quickly reunited and introduced to their non-Goan girlfriends. Fred's companion is Maria from Spain; Francis' is Ingeborg from Sweden; Jacob's is Carmen from Portugal; and George's is Frieda from Germany. I admit, it was all quite the surprise, especially with my mother's words ringing in my ears; warning me about Goans leaving their diplomas behind in favour of white girls.

"Most European girls are here in London as *au pairs*," Linda explains. "Life for young girls is very restrictive in Europe, so they come here as students, nurses, au pairs or part-time nannies."

"Lando, I've invited your old buddy, Tony, from Dr. Ribeiro's Goan School to join us," Fred says. "He was anxious to see you again... but you should know that he's going through a rough time. He's feeling very lonesome and rather sad."

Tony hung out with the rest of us kids at the Goan Gymkhana in Nairobi. He was always a happy kid and now he's a respected teacher, living in London. I can't imagine why he would be sad.

Francis joins in: "Our group has been living here for over a year and we're still settling in, but for the most part, we're all happy here. We were part of the last exodus from Nairobi in 1963 before Independence and we have no intention of going back to Kenya."

Jacob then offers his account. "My dad lost his job in Kenya. They wouldn't issue him a work permit that would allow him to stay. And with so much unrest, he really wanted to get my sisters out of there; so we all immigrated to the UK. Thankfully, I get to finish university and stay here. I hope you're not thinking of going back, Lando?"

I feel somewhat defensive. "I have ideas for housing the poor that I want to put to the test in Kenya. In any case, it's my country. I was born there and see no reason not to die there."

"The reason might be, there's no future for us brown folks now after *Uhuru*," Fred says.

George interjects. "I had no choice. In January, after the Massacre in Zanzibar, I found myself stateless. I was at Med School in Makerere, Kampala and carrying an older British Protectorate Passport, so I wasn't allowed to return. My uncle found me a family in Nairobi who put me up for a few weeks, and from there I got a visa to enter the UK. By the way, Lando, do you remember Hazel Pinto?" You met her at the Royal Tech student visit to Makerere."

"Sure," I replied.

"Did you know that her Grandfather and mine both got

to Zanzibar in 1872? And then she and I both landed in Mombasa." George continues. "I haven't heard from her and now with so many people's lives disrupted, I worry about what might have happened to her."

"Ah, here's Tony." Fred makes the necessary introductions.

In seconds, the band strikes up and all the couples abandon Tony and me as they rush to the dance floor. Tony regales me with his stories about a happy and active life in 1962, teaching and playing sports in Nakuru after graduating from College in Nairobi. He tells me, when his scholarship came through for a post-grad two-year stay in Britain, all hell broke loose.

He's clearly handsome and articulate; no doubt a prize catch within the Goan community, so it was hard to understand how such a privileged man could have a problem. But the problem soon became clear to me.

The family of a girl he was dating, coerced him into a swift marriage. It was so last minute, he returned from the honeymoon just forty-eight hours before departing for Heathrow. Now, he's faced with the dilemma of two years of celibacy. He didn't dare dance at the Palais, in case it would generate some malicious gossip that would reach the folks back home.

I attempt to lighten the mood. "Tony, thank God you're not a priest who has to endure a lifetime of celibacy." Then I ask the obvious question. "But why don't you just bring your wife here?"

"I'm working on it." He replies, "There's certainly no

future for bringing up kids in Kenya."

When we get home, Linda and David are curious to know more about what happened in Zanzibar that led to a massacre. They admit they were completely unaware of the events. So I give them a condensed version of history beginning in January, when the Africans, who were for centuries subjugated by the occupying Arabs, went on a rampage. They raped Arab and Asian women, looted homes, and murdered with abandon. They finally drove out the Arabs with the help of Tanganyika armed forces. Then after months of chaos, Tanganyika and Zanzibar forged a Union, which is how Tanzania was born. Many Goan families who had lived there and held important positions for almost seventy years, also fled."

"This is what worries me about Kenya." Linda says. "Can't you persuade Dad to emigrate as well? We could reunite our family here in the UK where life is so civilized."

"He'll never budge. And just so you know, like Dad, I will also stay in Kenya."

* *

Shortly after our amazing New Year's holiday, I'm on the train headed back to Liverpool.

The constant refrain that plays in my mind as the locomotive chugs along is: 'there's no future for Goans in Kenya. They're happy in Britain.' But I can't reconcile this with the anti-immigrant sentiments splashed all over the newspaper headlines. Perhaps it is the Goan capacity to adapt and integrate. After four hundred and fifty years of Portuguese colonial rule, of which two hundred were under the gruesome

Inquisition, this small community had been transformed and had lost their Indian roots. All they had to do was attend Mass at their local Catholic church, and the all-embracing welcome of some who had arrived earlier, would ensure they were not alone. To non-Goan parishioners and especially the clergy, they were a Godsend. They were delighted by the new arrivals as attendance at services had been steadily slipping. Judging by the harsh headlines everywhere, other brown and black immigrants were having a difficult time.

The measured clickety-clack of the train lulls me into a dream-like state in which my memory becomes focused on our New Year's Eve visit with Rachel, a friend of Linda's.

Rachel, who is busy preparing for our celebration, suddenly realizes she's out of cat food. Since everyone else was busy helping out, Linda suggests I go to the corner store and fetch some. I bundle up to face the cold, and just as I'm heading out the door, Rachel calls out, "Lando, please can you also get us a stick of French bread?"

The little old English lady at the cash desk, rings up the two small cans of cat-food and the bread. I pay, but as I turn to leave, she beckons me closer and whispers. "Sir, you do understand that this canned food is for cats?" I look at her blankly until it dawns on me that she's been reading the horrid 'Paki-bashing' tabloids. I smile and assure her: "Yes, Madam." I wave the bread in the air. "This is for me." Then I hold up a can... "And this is for the cat. Thank you for the warning though. Happy New Year!"

The train pulls into the station and I'm wide awake.

7

Assassination in Kenya

It is wet, cold and dark; altogether miserable as I trudge my way back home past the Philharmonic's frosted windows. Navigating down Mt. Pleasant is treacherous as the pavement has been dug up and heavy rains have turned it to mud.

I finally reach home and hang up my dripping overcoat in the vestibule with the rest of the residents' soggy outerwear.

There's a letter in my pigeonhole from my Dad who rarely writes. I take it and rush upstairs to read it.

March 1, 1965.

Dear Lando, I know this will come as a shock to you, but your hero, Pio Gama Pinto, is dead. It happened a few days ago. They buried him this afternoon at the City Park Cemetery. It was a very crowded funeral. All the politicians were there, as well as the whole Goan community.

Outrageous as it may seem... the fact is, he was murdered. Many are wondering if the new Independent Kenya is sending a message to Goans that it is time for us to leave this country.

I sit on the bed, light headed, my heart racing, my hand shaking... but I must read to the end.

Mum heard the news first last week from Uncle Antonio who received a call from Albert De Souza, who works with Pio's wife, Emma, at Wilson Airport. Emma was rushed away with a police escort. According to early newspaper reports, Pio was taking his daughter Tereska to school and waiting for the askari to open the gate. Three Africans drove up in a car. One man got out, came to the driver's side, greeted him as if he knew him, and shot him in the head. All three fled.

Fitz De Souza, a very good friend of Pio's, is helping Emma and the family through this nightmare. Of course, there are rumours and speculation. Some think it may have been the British and Americans behind the killing. They would like to purge Kenya of any communist or socialist thinking as they have major investments in this country. Pio was a close advisor to Jaramogi Oginga Odinga. According to rumour, 'Prisons' Azavedo, whom you also know, was heard telling Antonio Pinto at the funeral that the matata may have been initiated from within Kenyatta's own cabinet. There are rumours that a very angry President Kenyatta and Pio had an exchange of words in public, at the Parliament Building, just a day earlier. Some people think, as Speaker of the House, Fitz may know more, but he is keeping his mouth shut as lawyers usually do. When I have more news, I will send it to you. I know this is upsetting for you, son, but please do not let it interfere with your studies.

I'm devastated. I lie on the bed pressing my palms against the sides of my head to calm the throbbing. The images of Pio and the milestones in my life, flash by like a speeding silent film.

I recall one day, when my friend Savio and I interrupted our Ping-Pong game to investigate some raised voices coming from the bar at the Goan Gymkhana. Pio was shouting, trying to convince members that the only solution was a free and liberated Goa. "What is good for Goa is good for our Kenya. People must fight for their rights. The colonial rulers should be sent home."

I was only thirteen years old, but I felt I understood what Pio was saying when he talked about the desperate conditions of the poor: no water, no sanitation... no basic services.

I remember the collective shock that stunned the Goan community in 1954, when Pio Gama Pinto, Makan Sigh and others who had dared to speak out about social injustice, were picked up in the aftermath of *'Operation Anvil'* and incarcerated for years without a trial. But I also recall the elation we felt when we heard that Pio was released from prison and returned with his wife and two children to live a normal life in Nairobi.

I can't imagine why someone from within the new government would want to assassinate Pio. He was popular and instrumental in setting up the *Sauti Ya KANU* (Voice of KANU) for the Kenya African National Union. It was at Jomo Kenyatta's insistence in 1963, at Independence, that Pio was elected a Member of the Central Legislative Assembly. A year later, in July of 1964, he was appointed a Specially Elected Member of the House of Representatives.

It just doesn't add up. We can only hope, when they arrest his assassin, the full story will emerge.

* *

I look at my watch. I've missed dinner. I put on my dank overcoat and venture out into the cold wet night to comfort myself again with fish and chips.

When I return, I send Dad a brief note, thanking him for writing and I ask for more information when he has it.

* *

March 10, 1965, another letter arrives. According to Dad, Stephen has not turned up for a second month to collect his allowance:

"The last time he came by was just before Christmas; he brought a live jogoo (cock) as a gift from his mother. Mum had prepared gifts for his family that included two handmade dresses, a set of coloured pencils, and some of your sister Fatima's old story books. Stephen was happy with the money you sent and… I added fifty shillings. I'm pleased to read this revelation since Dad was generally tight with his money. The letter continues: *Mum gave him a small bag from her Cusuada (traditional homemade Goan Christmas sweets). Stephen said he remembered her making those sweets when he lived here. But during the short visit, he seemed very distracted or frightened about something. Mum and I are worried. Can you remember where he said they live now? Mum thinks it was Banana Hill, near Limuru, but we need something more definite. If I can get the address, I will persuade Ahmad to drive us there on a weekend. We do not wish to worry you, as we know you are diligently applying yourself to your studies.*

'There are rumours that more Goans will be losing their civil service jobs, as the new Government must give priority to Africans.

Otherwise, all is well. Do not worry. There will always be work for professionals like you. Keep well. Have you met any 'beetles' yet? Please drop a few lines to say you're well and safe.'

I head downstairs to dinner. I pick at my food and return directly to my room. The news of Stephen has unsettled me. It's all so strange, that ten years after his disappearance in 1954, Stephen reappears on the day of my departure.

I lie awake replaying the images of seven-year old Stephen as I last remember him, zooming around on his bicycle and skidding to a stop with a big smile. "Happy day, Lando!" he would shout day after day.

"You too, Stephen," I would reply. "No matata today, please."

8

A Year of Discovery

It's the end of the summer of '65. It's only been a year since my arrival in the UK but it feels like a lifetime. Nigel, a friend and English urban planning colleague and I have just returned from an eventful three-week trek across Europe to Greece. Nigel had spent time in Kenya with his parents in the mid-fifties, but our paths had not actually crossed back then, which was not surprising, given the racial segregation policies in place at the time. He loved the stupendous beauty of the landscape and adventure of safaris, and generally growing up, albeit briefly, in Kenya. It seemed natural that we would form a close connection. Since he majored in Geography at the University of Aberystwyth, I happily left the itinerary of our trip in his capable hands.

We planned on hitchhiking, but with greatly discounted student fares, we could afford to switch to trains and buses. Our initial ultimate destination was Asia. We wanted to leave our footprints on the eastern bank of the Bosporus Strait in Turkey; but since our budget didn't allow, we settled on Greece.

Travelling through cities that had existed for hundreds of years in Europe, compared to my experience in British East Africa, was an education for me. Nigel was a great guide.

"Much has been done since the rebuilding after WW2 to improve planning," Nigel says. "All governments, certainly in Western Europe, are giving more attention to careful management of land use; ensuring towns and hamlets are clustered to take maximum advantage of serviced land; and to maximize and preserve agricultural land."

"The great preoccupation must also be with the onslaught of motorcars," I say. We had both attended lectures on the impact of car-ownership on American cities. We talk about the different styles of architecture as we clickety-clack our way towards the frontier of the Eastern European countries.

There is a noticeable tension as we cross through Hungary and Yugoslavia with militarized border control personnel boarding trains in the middle of the night and demanding to see our passports and money. They return our passports, but keep the money. Fortunately, we were clever enough to have hidden most of our cash, not in our socks, as we had been advised by a colleague, but deep in the lining of our sleeping bags. The experience only increased our desire and anxiety to get to Greece.

In Athens, we head for a youth hostel near the Acropolis.

"We made it! I can't believe we're actually here," Nigel exclaims, as we both ease our backpacks onto a bench. Our rooftop lodgings offer panoramic views of the metropolis and for two US dollars a night, we can sleep under the stars.

"Fantastic," I say. "I don't care to be on a train again for a while."

We spend the next three days exploring tourist sites in the blazing heat. We sip water in the shade and enjoy simple Greek food like lamb *kleftiko*, octopus, chicken *kebabs*, *papoutsakia*, *fassolakia*, and wash it all down with *Retsina*: a white wine that got its name from the sealing of wine containers with a resin from the Aleppo pine tree. It's a bit salty to the taste… but it's plentiful, and more importantly… it's cheap.

On our last night, Nigel and I decide to visit a wine festival in the Plaka district. For a modest fee we each purchase an empty beaker so we can move around tasting a variety of more favourable wines. The mouth-watering scent of rosemary, oregano and roast lamb is everywhere. The path home is all-downhill along flagstone and clay tile-paved lanes crowded with sidewalk diners. The buildings behind, form a backdrop of contrasting colours. Clusters of planters are overflowing with giant bougainvillea in pink, mauve, orange and white. It's a magnificent, multi-sensory experience.

Nigel and I are in a 'happy' frame of mind. The sound of Bouzouki music fills the air. The rhythmic clapping of hands mixing with the sounds of happy voices seems to float out of every open window and door. More seductive are the muffled and more often amplified sounds that emanate from every other building. I imagine a thousand Zorbas dancing in those paved internal courtyards, open to the sky. We had visited some of them in daylight. Whitewashed walls and aquamarine door and window frames, setting off the bougainvillea and grapevine creepers in reds and greens. Pots of basil, rosemary and other herbs dotted around. The temptation is too much.

"What about a last one for the road?" Nigel says with a grin.

"Yes, let's."

"You go in first," he grins as he pushes me forward. I place my hand on one side of the blue double doors. They are unlocked. I trip, on the short landing that leads, a few steps below, to the courtyard. Nigel stumbles forward on top of me; almost a hundred and seventy pounds of him on my hundred and thirty pounds of bones. A burst of clapping and a tremendous cheer goes up from the assembled crowd. Perhaps they think we're part of the entertainment for the evening. Nigel, white complexion, six-foot-two, a mop of brown hair… and then there's me; brown-skinned, a mere five-feet-seven inches, with a black Beatle mop of hair. But what we both have in common are our goatee beards.

A man, obviously the host, happily greets us with open arms. "I'm Spyros," he says with a handshake. We introduce ourselves.

He seems delighted to hear I was born in Kenya. "Wonderful. I was born in Tanganyika. Come… you must join us." He signals the waiter to add two chairs to his table. "*Karibu*. Welcome again! You never forget the land of your birth."

He tells us his father ran a farm in Tanganyika, but returned to Greece with his family after World War One when

Spyros was six-years old.

Spyros tells us why he is so happy today. It seems we are guests at the wedding reception for his only daughter, Katharina. They are a truly beautiful couple who will be flying to Zanzibar for their honeymoon.

Spyros had spent his lifetime dreaming of returning to Africa one day. "I cannot travel now, so Katharina will go for me. *Karibu.* So welcome to you both, on this wonderful occasion! There is *Ouzo*, *Retsina* and red wine in abundance. So drink up my friends." He fills our glasses and we willingly oblige.

* *

Over the next two days Nigel and I take day trips by ferry from the Greek port of Piraeus, to the islands of Hydra and Spetses. Both are island communities whose people live very much as they have for centuries. They walk everywhere and use donkey carts to move their loads around. They survive on tourism, especially as both are destinations for sailing enthusiasts. Sleek yachts and other craft, crowd around the docks. A cruise ship is anchored off shore.

The next morning, we travel by bus again, this time with our backpacks, to Piraeus where we catch a passenger ferry that is packed to capacity. We sleep on the deck while it glides through the Corinth Canal and on to the Italian port of Brindisi. There is plenty of time to talk. Inevitably, the subject of Kenya comes up. Nigel waxes nostalgically of his stay. "Like you Lando, my time in Africa shaped me. At the time, I thought it would be disruptive for my education, but now looking back, I know my Dad was right. Travel broadens the mind more than anything else."

"How old were you then?"

"Eleven and my brother was nine. It was over the period from 1953-1957 during the Mau Mau Emergency. Dad was a Telecommunications Engineer and seconded by his employer Standard Telephones, to the RAF at Eastleigh Airport. He didn't say much to us about what he did, but Eastleigh was where all the British troops were flown during the emergency."

"Did the Mau Mau affect you?"

"No, not directly. I remember Dad being in the Home Guard and going on patrol at night along the Nairobi River which ran behind where we lived in Westlands."

"That's not too far from where we live in Plums Lane, opposite the Parklands Sports Club. The Nairobi River meanders parallel to Riverside Drive, under Ainsworth Bridge, past the Coryndon Museum and behind the Norfolk Hotel on its way to Ngara. It's by the bridge that my high school friend Savio and I saw our first dead man. I think the police shot him and left him to die in the tall grass. It was horrible. The flies and the smell."

"I still remember the barbed wire everywhere. My brother and I went to Westlands Primary and then to the Prince of Wales. That was like a prison with barbed wire around the perimeter. I vividly remember *Operation Anvil* and the whole city coming to a standstill," Nigel says.

"I remember that day too. Savio and I had gone to our

school as usual. When I returned home, my mother was in a state of shock. The police and troops had raided all the servants' quarters in Nairobi for Kikuyu suspects who may have links to the Mau Mau. They took away Mwangi, our houseboy, his wife, their seven-year-old son and two-year-old daughter. They all spent years in a detention village. The family never saw their father again. Stephen, the son, finally found his way back to our home ten years later. He's about nineteen now. He has never received access to even primary education, and is trying to take care of his mother and sister."

"That's very sad. I can't say I'm proud of our colonial history."

"It's not over yet," I caution. "I feel as if the chickens of colonialism are coming home to roost via Heathrow Airport. I was surprised when I landed in the UK, to see the anti-coloured immigration headlines in local newspapers.

"Did you live all the time in Westlands, Nigel?"

"No. We moved to Spring Valley and then to Karen. Housing was difficult and expensive, so we rented furnished houses whilst the owners were on leave in the UK. We also looked after their pets, which was good fun, particularly in Karen where we had eleven acres of *shamba* (land) to roam. However, other than a gardener, we did not have staff. Neither my father nor mothers were comfortable with employing servants. I think our white Kenyan neighbours, *Mzungus*, thought us odd."

"I suppose I have always seen the employment of servants as an opportunity of employment for local people. Our community did not have the income levels to support more than one person, and sometimes shared the cost of a gardener between two families."

"Did you know Mayor Ronnie Alexander? He was an 'Old Boy' of the school in 1956. He invited us to welcome the Queen Mother on her visit to Kenya."

"Been there, done that! Our school had us hike in the hot sun to line up along the Princess Elizabeth Highway (Uhuru Highway) to welcome the then Princess Elizabeth and Prince Philip in 1952, and then trot off to State House for a piece of cake. She became Queen while she was up at Treetops Lodge in Nanyuki.

"Did you go on any safaris?"

"Dad used to drive us in his Morris Oxford to Mombasa for our summer holidays. He liked the tarmac roads in Tanganyika so we drove across the Athi Plains to the border, staying at the Lake Manyara Hotel in Arusha, and then drove back into Kenya via Voi, where we had High Tea at the railway station. Afterward it was on to Mombasa to stay at the Shelly Beach Hotel. Mombasa was so relaxed after the tensions of Nairobi. We did a number of trips to Tsavo National Park and Mzima Springs."

"Would you go back?" I ask.

"Like a shot," he says. "Though I'll wait until you're back there because I'm sure I will see a different Kenya through your eyes. Remember, I was taken only to spots safe for the Mzungus… and I should tell you that I really resented being called Mzungu. Overall, I loved living in Kenya."

The next morning we awaken before dawn. A thin silver line appears to separate a dark ultramarine sea from a deep orangey-purple sky.

Minutes later we disembark, grab a quick breakfast, and catch a bus to the Swiss border at Como.

Of one thing, we are certain... we are completely broke.

About 1:30 P.M. we depart the bus station near the Como San Giovanni train station and set off on foot out of Italy. We think we will head for Geneva. We could not have planned for a more beautiful afternoon to be outdoors. The crisp, clear mountain air is invigorating. In every direction lush green countryside reverberates into panoramic vistas that fade into distant blue-grey silhouettes. There is little movement on the road. In the silence of the natural beauty around us, even the distant purr of an engine is amplified. A car zooms by dangerously close. I jump from a rough grassy shoulder into a ditch. Nigel follows. The driver sticks his hand out of the window and gives us the 'bird'. Nigel's hand goes up with fingers crossed for good luck and we mumble some choice expletives, but it's too beautiful a day to worry about one miscreant.

I arise from the ditch just in time to spot a cherry red convertible sports car with its top down approaching. Our hands are waving frantically, our thumbs erect, in the hope we'll be noticed... and we are. We straighten ourselves up and smile brightly.

The two young ladies slow down and stop. "Okay, you have our attention, so what can we do for you?"

"Maybe give us a ride as far as you are going... if you're

going toward Geneva that is?" Nigel flashes an extra wide smile which I try to match.

"No pardone," the driver says. "We go to Basle. We can arrive in three hour. If you want to go, please you may to come with us."

Nigel looks at me, we nod and climb into the back seat for the fun ride of our lives. We try to make light conversation, but at the speed we're travelling, some words make it while others just float away on a cloud of incoherence.

The girls are gracious to the end. They drop us off at the train station; and sadly, we're too broke to even offer them a drink.

We spend the weekend sleeping on benches at the Basle Railway Station waiting until Monday for the banks to open and wire us money.

Sunday morning provides us with a firsthand look at the cultural difference between the Swiss and British towns. Basle is a meticulously clean Medieval Town on the banks of the Rhine River. There is almost no outdoor advertising allowed. Every bush, shrub and lawn is groomed to perfection. They even seem to manage to make their garbage invisible. Surely they must generate some?

Monday morning we are waiting outside a Bank, just before opening time. Nigel and I are clean-shaven and doing our best to look as spruced up as is possible after sleeping on rail station benches for two nights. Nigel convinces me that I should be the one to go in and do the talking, while he waits with the two backpacks. "I'll explain later," he tells me.

I take a deep breath and head inside to survey the area. At the entrance, I take notice of a brass plaque that begins with… *manager*. I copy it down and head back out to show it to Nigel: *Manager, 'Monsieur Boulanger'*. I try pronouncing the name with a French accent. Now I 'confidently' approach the receptionist.

"Good Morning, Madame, I am here to see Monsieur Boulanger, the Manager," I announce politely but firmly.

"Is he expecting you?"

"I hope so," I reply.

She summons an underling; a smartly attired and coiffured young lady, who escorts me into a dedicated elevator. I am whisked up to a marbled lobby outside the Manager's luxurious penthouse office on the 5th Floor. The cabin of the elevator has the intoxicating aroma of freshly smoked cigars.

She gently opens the outer door to an ante-room and signals me to proceed through the next doorway, which leads me into the opulent office. The walls are decorated with magnificent oil paintings. I recognize one by the famous artist Ferdinand Leger.

M. Boulanger is seated behind his desk. He rises and walks around to welcome me like an old friend. I extend my hand to accept his welcome. I see him hesitate for a moment, as if he was expecting someone else.

I introduce myself and explain to him how we had to involuntarily share part of our cash with the border guards in Hungary and Yugoslavia and that we are completely broke and need money wired urgently from Liverpool.

He attempts a forced grin. It is obvious he is not amused. He calls out to his Secretary in the outer office and explodes in angry French. She immediately summons an errand-boy. M. Boulanger ushers me to his doorway. "He will take you to the cashier. Goodbye." He begins to close the door before I've barely passed through it.

The office boy walks me onto a much less opulent public elevator that descends faster than Superman in flight. We exit together and he leads me along a corridor to a cashier. I fill out the appropriate paperwork and make a speedy departure.

Nigel bursts out laughing as I recount my experience. "I bet they assumed you to be a princeling of a wealthy Indian or Arab family, or even a foreign politician, wishing to deposit funds into a secret account. That is what they do best, hence the VIP treatment at first, and if you disappoint, they treat you like a pile of manure. You are worth nothing here if you're broke."

"Your father was right. Travel broadens the mind," I reply. "Let's hope the money arrives quickly."

The wire transfer arrived the next morning.

9

A Stronger Cuppa

September 1965.

The trip was marvelous but I'm relieved and happy to be back at the University.

In the Common Room, the mid-afternoon sun is streaming in and in its glow, I glimpse Eleanor Pearson curled up in the armchair, reading once again.

I offer her a cuppa.

Instead of her past 'No thank you, I'm full up on tea,' she surprises me.

"Yes, please. I'd love one. Thank you." She's cheerful. As the tea steeps, a brief news item in the *Liverpool Echo* catches my attention. It relates to the release of three persons who had been detained after scuffles broke out at the recent Orange Parade. I take the tea and the newspaper to Eleanor.

"Eleanor, can you please explain why you Protestants are still trying to kill off us Catholics?" I tease, pointing to the news item.

"Because you're troublemakers… and there are too many of you, anyway," she says grinning. "Have you ever attended the Orange Parade?"

I tell her that during my first week in Liverpool, Nelson saw the announcement in the newspaper. I offer up my best and silliest Nelson impression: 'Lando, we go to parade. It like Rio Carnival. We will go to enjoy. You please to come with me? My *Ingleesh* not good, so okay, you come please, yes?' Eleanor smiles.

"So we took the bus and trusted the driver to let us know where to get off. There was no need, because from the bus window we could see and hear hundreds of people lined up on either side of the street, waving banners, posters and flags, and shouting some nasty slogans to those on the opposite side of the street. There was a man standing on a wooden crate flapping his hands wildly and hollering into a megaphone to enthusiastic cheers from the assembled crowd."

"You could have gotten yourselves into a lot of trouble," Eleanor surmises.

"We quickly realized that. Many stores were boarded up, yet there were pubs open on every corner. We walked for about three blocks, past pawnshops, used clothing and second-hand furniture stores. Because the Europeans in Kenya were all so rich, I never imagined I would see such poverty in England."

"We're still paying for past wars, that's why Britain had to give up its Empire," she says gleefully. "So did you leave?"

"Yes. A butcher was standing in the doorway of his shop. He pulled us aside and in his heavy Irish brogue, intimated that we should leave the area immediately. He said the place would soon get bloody rowdy. We listened well and then caught the next bus back to Mount Pleasant. Nelson was not amused. He said 'British people must to visit Brazil at Carnival to learn to make a good parade.'"

"Much of that poverty you witnessed was a result of immigration," Eleanor says. "Following the Irish potato famine in 1847, thousands of Irish came to Liverpool desperate to find work and there was none to be had, so the next step was to try and emigrate to America or Canada. The many that didn't manage to get on a ship, stayed here. Some of my ancestors were among them. Large areas of Liverpool became ghettos of agricultural workers trapped in an urban economy."

"That is exactly what the 'foreign experts' are predicting will happen now in Nairobi and other big towns. Thousands of Africans, who previously worked on European farms, have begun to pour in from the countryside looking for work. Before, there were laws controlling the movement of Africans to the towns and cities. The experts predict the urban population will grow very rapidly. I wonder if one day, Nairobi and other urban centres will have open conflict on their streets."

Eleanor takes a sip of her cold tea. "The Annual Orange Parade is the one day every year when Protestants remind the Catholics that they were once crushed in a battle almost three hundred years ago by William of Orange. How are you on British history?"

"Not much on detail," I reply.

"Don't worry, you'll be safe. No one will even suspect you of being Catholic," she flippantly adds.

To casually change the subject, I decide to tell her all

about my trip with my friend Nigel.

"Our goal was Turkey and Asia Minor; but after the border guards helped themselves to our money, we realized we'd never get that far, so we headed for Greece instead.

"Ah, it's also been my dream to visit Turkey and Asia Minor," she says. She checks her watch. "Gosh, I must go. But please let's meet again. I want to hear more." We shake hands and separate.

I'm pleasantly surprised at how easy it has been to talk with Eleanor today. Now that the ice of shyness has been chipped away, I know we'll meet and talk again.

That evening, I find myself replaying my conversation with Eleanor in my head. I'm baffled about the Irish fighting over religion. My Goan community in Kenya received almost all our moral and spiritual guidance in the Catholic churches and schools that were invariably staffed by Irish priests and nuns. They always preached peace and forgiveness and turning the other cheek.

When my friend Jeep and I were little, we used to help Ahmad wash his taxicab while he plied us with stories of years ago. He insisted that, "People will stay angry with each other for centuries over religious differences." Of course, he was referring to the bloody massacres in India and Pakistan following Independence from Britain in 1947.

Ahmad recalled how, soon after their marriage, he was separated for months from his wife Serena, simply because their families lived on different sides of the border. If it's not ethnic or racial conflict, it's religious.

* *

The following week, Eleanor and I meet again and discuss our favourite movies. One in particular was *Lawrence of Arabia*, a film about English Lieutenant T.E. Lawrence who is sent to Arabia to meet with Prince Faisal, hoping to seek his help in uniting Arab factions to support the British in their fight against the Turks during World War I. Eleanor speaks glowingly of her favourite actors, Peter O'Toole who plays Lawrence, and Omar Sharif who plays Lawrence's Bedouin Guide, Sharif Ali. We agree, it's a magnificently directed movie, set against an incredible desert landscape, and it provides an interesting insight into history. It's clear to me; we must go to more movies together.

A week later, we meet at The Liverpool Philharmonic, a pub near the University. Eleanor tells me about her childhood. "I was a wartime baby, so when my father was on active duty overseas, Mummy moved in with my grandparents. It was a great arrangement for me, as both grandparents and my Aunt Nancy doted on me. I was young then, but as I grew older, I realized it was a period of great uncertainty. After the D-Day landings, we didn't know whether Daddy was alive or dead. Thankfully, he returned to us whole."

"How many children… I mean… siblings… do you have?"

"Just one. My brother, Edward, who arrived in 1947. He was a cute baby and I treated him like a doll. But I felt quite early on that my mother was letting him get away with murder, so-o… I kind of took charge of his upbringing. I'm proud to say, he's grown into a lovely young man that I love so much."

I smile. "I think I'm kind of like Edward. I have a sister, Linda, only three years older than me. She kept me on a tight leash until I became a teenager. Then things changed. My parents wouldn't let her go to parties without a chaperone. So, I became her designated chaperone. There's power in that."

"Where does she live now?"

"In London."

"Oh. Do you have any other siblings?"

"I do. I have three brothers and two sisters."

Eleanor tells me about her later years at Stourbridge High School where she excelled at academic studies but was extremely talented at athletics like, netball, hockey and tennis.

"Then why did you choose sociology?"

"My mother was very involved in social work. There was a lot of poverty around the Midlands after the war. German bombs demolished parts of Birmingham, Coventry, Manchester and Liverpool, places that were already depressed economically. Jobs had disappeared and there was urban blight everywhere. I was competing for a County scholarship, so I opted for something that might be useful. I won the scholarship and was happy to arrive in Liverpool. Why not? It has the Beatles and the best Liverpool pop groups."

"Did you find the course useful?"

"Loved it. I believe it changed the way I think."

"How so?"

"Well, I was brought up in a conservative household where all my other relatives think the same way. It would get them really rattled when I would call them 'petit bourgeois.' I began to dream of a more just world. I became a supporter of the campaign for nuclear disarmament and went on 'Ban the Bomb' marches," she grins.

"And what made you choose planning?"

"The same sort of reasons, really. I wanted to use my talents to help build a more just society. I grew up in a colonial world, segregated by race, separated by religion, and stratified by economic and social class. I was always shocked by the living conditions of Africans and I wanted to change the type of housing that was being provided for them."

"That's an ambitious goal."

"Yes, especially when I kept applying for scholarships to go abroad, only to find that priority was always given to African students who were designated to take over government positions at Independence. But then, I won a design competition for Kenya's Independence Street Decorations, and suddenly, a scholarship offer came along and here I am."

"Destiny, I suppose." Eleanor sighs.

"Mum used to say that God has a plan for each of us… *'Que Sera, Sera'* to quote Doris Day. Dad was more pragmatic. 'Nobody owes you a living' was his favourite phrase. 'You've got to work hard and get through exams.' But thankfully, he also understood that boys need to have a little fun, occasionally."

"By the way, Lando, you talked about getting out of that Methodist hostel. If you still want to move, there's a vacancy coming up in our building. Are you interested?"

"Yes! Yes, I am." *Can you please find out how much I need*

for a deposit?"

10

Love Isn't Necessarily Black and White

Two weeks later, I'm in my new digs; a red brick Victorian house, a thirty-minute bus ride from the University. Four students share a tiny living room and kitchen and two toilets on the upper floor but each of us occupies a separate bedroom.

On my second day, as I unlock my room, I am viciously attacked from behind. A sharp instrument pierces my shirt. I drop my briefcase and cry out. Eleanor rushes from her room and takes in the scene. She observes the fear on my face and begins to laugh.

She points to a cat that is poised on the window ledge hissing and bristling with anger. "That's Solly… short for Solitude," she says. "I'm sorry. I should have warned you about her. She's definitely mentally disturbed. The owners live downstairs with their four prize-winning racing greyhounds that they dote on. It's evident they ignore the cat but keep her around to hunt any mice that might turn up."

"Look, I'm bleeding!" I lift my shirt and run my fingers over the claw marks. "It really stings. How do you deal with that crazy cat?"

"When I moved in last year, I took to feeding Solly, and I have to tell you, cat food's not cheap," Eleanor chuckles. "Anyway, she's gotten pretty attached to this food provider, so maybe she thinks you're here to take her sugar mommy away."

"Nah, it's probably just hunger. Listen, let me pay for her food from now on. I'm happy to share something from my taxpayer-funded scholarship to support society's marginalized cats. And maybe she'll sense that *I'm the hand that feeds her* and she'll treat me with more respect."

Maybe it was my noble gesture of offering sustenance for the starving cat, or maybe it was empathy over my feline battle wounds; whatever it was, Eleanor and I saw a lot more of each other after that incident.

Our friendship develops into a pleasant routine that includes visits to art galleries, eating out, movies, and discussions on music and current pop groups; and periodically, day trips to nearby towns like Chester and Birkenhead across the River Mersey.

We often drift into discussions about politics and the potential of future social conflict in the country. The 'Winds of Change' policy has tides of immigrants, non-white British citizens and British Protected persons now arriving in their 'motherland.' Thousands had fought and died defending the Union Jack in faraway wars; and those generations in countries that were once integral constituents under the British Empire had been indoctrinated into believing they were 'British.' In turn, they swore their full allegiance to the Crown. After an imperial colonial presence of more than two centuries, the two major political parties held opposing views on how to address the issue.

"Most immigrants seem to want a British passport," she says. "Don't you?"

"Not for me," I reply. "I do not because I intend to return to Kenya."

On a chilly, blustery November evening, we are crouched in a corner of a bus shelter by the Philharmonic when Eleanor asks: "Lando, can we postpone our visit to the Grosvenor Museum in Chester next Saturday?" I was startled because I hadn't known her to change plans before. She carefully explains: "Margaret thinks John is getting serious about their relationship and she'd like our opinion of him. So, I plan to cook a special dinner just for the four of us."

The dinner was an interesting success. Eleanor had prepared a spicy Indian curry with Basmati rice, and garnished the dish with delicately carved radishes, sweet peppers and carrots. I give her marks for sheer initiative. She had bought the right selection of spices at a small Indian grocery, however, she had misplaced the newspaper clipping of the recipe, so her measurements were off, which meant the heat was on. In traditional Indian meals, a sprinkling of an assorted yogurt mix will both enhance the individual taste of spices and douse the cumulative combustive heat of the chilies and peppers. But then Eleanor was not traditionally Indian.

In the end, we were unable to make the requested judgment, neither on John and Margaret's relationship, nor on their review of Indian culinary offerings. Though I did notice, they washed their meal down with great quantities of wine and water, and as a result they left looking extremely flushed and bloated.

* *

Eleanor unwittingly, challenges me to a kind of dinner duel. So, the following week I host a dinner for the two of us. Although I can cook a reasonable curry, I decide turnabout is fair play, therefore I will demonstrate my culinary prowess with a simple English recipe.

I cannot lie. It was not an impressive performance. The pork chops were dry and brittle, the over-boiled peas resembled mushed avocado, and the red cabbage, intended to bring colour to the presentation, was bleached to a pale pink.

Eleanor made a valiant attempt to nibble at the offering, but consoled me with the assurance that to replicate English cooking has proved challenging to more adventurous souls than me. "Most English people will admit that we generally start with good fresh ingredients, which we somehow manage to destroy during preparation." She blamed it on the depression years, WWII, and the widespread poverty that followed. "People were so very poor. Until the fifties, food was still being rationed, unless you were the landed gentry, who never seem to starve."

**

Weeks become months. Our friendship continues to develop and it seems we are falling in love.

We talk about our families. We discuss our previous relationships.

"I used to be quite pretty in high school. I had blonde silky hair and long slender legs… and I had lots of boyfriends. Then, at university I met this bloke, who I thought was rather attractive. We were getting to be pretty close, when he felt compelled to buy a ninety-nine dollar Greyhound Bus Package and travel around the USA and Canada. Poof, he never returned."

As Eleanor reminisces about her childhood crush, she seems to grow somewhat shy and aloof again, rather like when I first met her.

"Puppy love. Happens all the time," I interject, remembering the words my sister Linda used, to console me over memories of Saboti.

"You're probably right. Now, tell me about your first crush," Eleanor urges.

I tell her about Saboti. She listens attentively, then shrugs and smiles, "Puppy love… happens all the time," and she bursts into her unreserved giggle that I find so endearing.

In the weeks that follow, Eleanor tells me she is reading several books on Kenya. She loves adventure. She's convinced Kenya is a beautiful country and has concluded that the Maasai are a particularly handsome tribe. She admits hating to see animals caged, and thinks it would be lovely to be able to see wildlife roaming free in Kenya's national parks.

At some point, she begins to quiz me.

"Lando, did you know about Mr. Pooran Singh and his blacksmith's shop, mentioned in Karen Blixen's novel, *Out*

Of Africa? Oh, and did you know, in Alys Reece's book, *To My Wife - Fifty Camels*, that Mr. Fernandes was Goan, and he was the most famous trader in Marsabit in the 1930s?"

I did not know the answers to either of those questions, but she wasn't done yet.

"When his lorry wasn't packed with goods, Mr. Fernandes would fill it up with paying travellers. In the middle of the night, he would park his lorry by the side of the road and brew tea over an open campfire for his passengers before loading them back onto the vehicle to continue on the long, exhausting drive from Marsabit to Isiolo with his eyes half shut."

Knowing that Eleanor is keen on learning more about Kenya, I suggest some other books that I'd read: J H Patterson, *The Man-Eaters of Tsavo*; Joy Adamson, *Born Free*; Ernest Hemmingway, *Green Hills of Africa*; and Justus Strandes, *The Portuguese Period in East Africa*. Eleanor is delighted. She loves every book she reads about Kenya. I'm amazed and delighted she has the time for so much reading!

We fall deeply in love.

Within months, we conclude that we can't possibly live without each other. We resolve to marry immediately after graduation and we'll honeymoon in Turkey.

And to my relief, we both agree we will make Kenya our home.

Next, we must share the news with our families. We begin with a visit to London where Eleanor meets Linda and David and their two-year old son, Paul. They all fall in love with her. As we are leaving, Paul is at the door with his little travel bag. He wants to go to Liverpool with Eleanor.

Then, we visit my Uncle Renato and his wife, Mavis, in their new home in Mill Hill. Uncle Renato shares with us the events that led to his sudden arrival in the UK. He had immigrated to Kenya from Goa in 1955. He was an engineer employed at the International Aeradio (IA) at Wilson Airport. In 1960, he was sent to the UK for further training at their parent company; and on his return to Kenya, he was promoted to Chief Engineer. Renato married Mavis in 1963 as a surge of emigrants were fleeing the country prior to Uhuru.

"I thought I was pregnant. My family had already left for the UK and I was not willing to stay in Kenya a day longer," Mavis firmly states. "It was not a safe place to raise a family. Your uncle loved his job and Kenya, almost equally, so if I'd not taken a stand, he would never have moved."

I glance at Eleanor to see if these negative comments might alter her eagerness to make our home in Kenya. She seems unperturbed and redirects the conversation. "What's the baby's name?"

"Well, we made a vow to the Blessed Virgin that we'd honour her for helping us get safely out of Kenya and settled in England. If we had a girl, we would call her Maria," Renato proudly declares.

"But," Mavis interjects, "*she* was a boy, so *he's* Mario!" She chuckles. She suddenly screws up her nose, picks up the baby, and heads out of the room, taking the aroma of baby poop with her.

As the evening goes on, my Uncle Renato has attached

himself to my Panasonic Super 8 movie camera. He makes me an offer. He and Mavis want to capture every minute of Mario's life, and he's willing to pay a fair price for the privilege. I know the cash will definitely help with our wedding plans. We have a deal.

* *

Two weeks later, it's my turn to meet Eleanor's parents.

Their home is in Wolverhampton, which is about a two-and-a half hour bus ride from Liverpool. En route, Eleanor prepares me for the meeting with a reminder of her brief family biography: Her dad inherited and manages their family furnishing business. His real loves are painting, fishing and music; and strange as it seems to me, his love for cars includes his own luxurious leather-upholstered Jaguar. Eleanor's mother retired as a teacher, but remains extremely busy as a volunteer with a number of social organizations.

Her mum and dad meet us at the station and drive us to their home on the outskirts of the city. It's a comfortable house in a typical middle class, well-treed suburb. The autumn colours are just turning on the ivy that covers one side of the house. A climbing rose engulfs the wooden trellis wall awaiting a final trim before settling in for the winter. My arrival appears to have excited the dog, a tan and white Cavalier King Charles Spaniel with his own distinct predisposition. We became 'sort of friends' by the end of the visit.

It's clear that Eleanor had asked that they spare me the discomfort of opening the conversation. So, during the visit, her mother begins and maintains a continuous commentary, sometimes catching me off-guard.

"Lando have you travelled to New Zealand?" she asks.

"No, not yet," I reply. "I would love to do so one day." It occurs to me that perhaps she thinks New Zealand is somewhere on the way to Kenya.

"I was told that sheep there outnumber the people population by about 15 to 1," her mother continues.

Aha, I was wrong! I think her mother is trying to ferret information on whether I'm a vegetarian? M-m. All I can think about now is how much I love lamb chops. She has no way of knowing that Goans eat all sorts of food. We have no taboos on beef, pork, lamb or poultry.

"Mummy, please tell Lando about your Indian family doctor," Eleanor tries to deflect her mother's comments. "You know Grandpa's friend with the little chubby son. He'll love that story. I tried to tell it but I can't tell it as well as you."

During the course of the visit we cover a number of diverse topics that include: social issues in the UK, my family background, and a critique of my experience after two years of living in Britain.

All-in-all, we had a lovely weekend with our gracious hosts. As we waved goodbye at the bus station, Eleanor and I took heart in the fact that we all emerged from the 'meet and greet' unscathed. All happily content with our pending union, and respectful of each other's differences… even if I still can't understand how a man can love a car so much.

As the bus pulls away, I exhale a sigh. "Well, thankfully, they were really excited," I conclude.

Eleanor suggests, "My dear Lando, your assessment of their excitement may be a bit premature."

I'm surprised that Eleanor is fostering doubt.

But then, upon our return to Liverpool, Eleanor is summoned to return home the following weekend for another visit… alone.

* *

After an interminable weekend without Eleanor, she returns to me. I'm riddled with anxiety while she is remarkably calm.

"So how did it go?" I ask in as cool a voice as I can muster.

"Well, as you know, my folks are conservative. They need time to adjust to new ideas."

"What's new about marriage?" I ask. "People have been marrying for centuries."

"It's just that mixed race marriages are not yet common in England, and they seem worried about causing a scandal among their circle of friends.

"What!" I do my best to control myself. "Scandal? Okay. So, how did you respond?"

"I reminded them about my Aunt Nellie, who we stayed with for a time toward the end of the war. She was a widowed music teacher, with two young children living in Wimbledon. She ran away with a married man and what was even more scandalous? They remained together, unmarried until his death. This news was kept secret from Aunt Nellie's kids until it was revealed after her death, a few years ago.. Fortunately, they were mature enough to accept it, with a bit of humour.

The world is changing."

"So were your parents okay after that bit of quick thinking?"

"Yes. It seemed to calm them. Mummy suggested we marry immediately after graduation. But at all costs, she instructs, we must stay away from Kenya and the Mau-Mau... even if it means we have to emigrate to Canada or New Zealand. She insists those are peaceful countries... and they love the Queen."

"That explains her comments about New Zealand and all those bloody sheep," I say. "I thought she wanted to find out if I could eat lamb. Your mum is a couple of steps ahead of us, and trying to brainwash us into emigrating to New Zealand."

"Please understand, Lando, although I know from what you've told me, the insurgency in Kenya ended ten years ago, those gruesome images that dominated our nightly TV news, are indelibly printed on their minds. Horrific Mau-Mau panga attacks on white settlers, their own black brothers, pregnant mothers, babies, old people and the disabled, were front page news. It isn't easy to convince my parents that Kenya is now a peaceful country under President Jomo Kenyatta."

"Thousands of British remained after Uhuru," I say. "Except for those that collected money for their farms and ran to South Africa and Australia."

"Also, Lando, Daddy suggests we wait six months before marriage."

"Six months? Why?"

"He says it will give you time to realize what a terrible

liability I can be."

I'm about to protest when she offers up one of her captivating giggles.

"Joking aside; Daddy's thinking is that after you've had time back home on your own, you might come to the conclusion that bringing me to Kenya isn't the best solution."

"I don't need time. Do you?"

"No, I don't. Daddy also wants us to be married in a Catholic church."

"But they're Anglican, so why a Catholic church?"

"He's never heard of Goa, or brown-skinned Catholics. So... he's suspicious that with your beard and long hair, you might really be a Muslim."

"Me a Muslim? Tell me you're joking!"

"No, I'm definitely not!" Eleanor replies firmly. "I know this is difficult for you, but please try to understand them. Since the war, their whole worldview is shaped by television. Whenever there's a plane hijacking or some other crazy attack, it's invariably, unshaven brown-skinned Muslims in the news. Those images are what they remember."

"So shall I shave my beard, cut my hair, get a blonde wig, or maybe dangle a crucifix from my neck before I meet them again?"

"No silly, I love you just as you are," Eleanor says with a reassuring smile. "By the way, I want you to know, I'm going to Kenya with or without you."

"Good answer!" I pull her close in a passionate embrace. "But you know what? I think waiting six months is not a bad idea. It'll give me a chance to arrange what's needed in Kenya for our wedding."

"No, wait, that's another thing!" Eleanor blushes. "They want us to be married *here* in England in six months, not Kenya."

"That might be an unresolvable obstacle for my parents."

"I don't understand. Why would it be a bigger problem for yours to come here than mine to go there?"

"My father has never been on a plane in his life, and will never get on a plane no matter what. Not even for one of their kids' weddings. He never has. And if he won't come, my mother won't either. It may also have to do with the exorbitant cost of air travel. No! They will not come. But to be honest, they won't stand in our way either. So we'll figure out a compromise that will make them happy when we get to Kenya."

"Okay, we'll figure it out. In the meantime, my darling, don't worry about the arrangements here, I'll handle it at this end. But can you calm the turbulence you're bound to find at your end of the world."

"I think that as long as we're having a Catholic wedding, my parents will be thrilled."

"Okay, I leave it in your capable hands."

"Good. So luv, will we still go ahead with our original honeymoon plans for Turkey in July?"

"Why should that change?" She looks at me bewildered.

"Well, my enlightened sweetheart, it's just that we'll be having our honeymoon before the wedding and in some cultures that's considered a sin. But if your family is okay with it, then…"

"Lando, you're the one who has to deal with all that Catholic guilt." She giggles.

"You're worth it." I grin, "But to be less confrontational; instead of a honeymoon, for my parents' sake, let's call it our Istanbul Safari."

With that quip, Eleanor agrees and rebounds with a reassuring question.

"So, Istanbul Safari it is. And we're okay with all this then?"

I take her in my arms and assure her that we are truly okay.

* *

The next few months are packed with finishing our studies and planning our trip.

A letter arrives from Kenya informing us that my parents understand that the wedding will be in England. They know that custom dictates the choice is generally left to the bride's side. However, the news of my return to Kenya to find a job and make arrangements for Eleanor's arrival has made my parents very happy, and the news that it will be a Catholic wedding has made them ecstatic.

11

Safari to Istanbul

Calais, July 24, 1966.

Eleanor and I make our way to a café to freshen up and recover from a rather jarring trip across the English Channel.

We had spent a lot of time over the past months poring over maps. Besides the three nights in Paris, our plan includes visiting specific places in Turkey, Greece and Italy; a sort of appetizer for future holidays.

In Paris, we stay in the Latin Quarter, where the Sorbonne and other educational institutions are concentrated. We want to experience the vibrant cultural life on the streets. We're not disappointed.

On the evening of July 26th, Paris seems to suddenly stop. Traffic has diminished. There's an unusual feel to the neighbourhood. People are standing outside of stores, gawking in the windows.

"Lando, I wonder what's happening?" Eleanor is first to express her anxiety. Two young men dash across the road towards us and head into a restaurant. They're wearing the red, green and gold of the Portuguese flag. The crowd at the storefront is glued to the TV screen.

I grab Eleanor's hand. "It's today! The finals!" We squeeze into the restaurant, already packed to capacity. Everyone is watching the FIFA World Cup soccer match being played at Wembley.

"This is the game my cousin Mario travelled from Lisbon to watch," I tell her, "and do you remember my Brazilian friend Nelson from the hostel? This is what he was dreaming about. I bet he's got a VIP seat out there." Portugal seems to have popular support against France's traditional rivals like England. With Eleanor at my side, I am somewhat conflicted about which side I should cheer for.

England beats Portugal 2-1. It's over. The crowd thins out. Some stay to celebrate. Others share and commiserate on Portugal's defeat and carry out a 'post mortem'. We continue our tour.

We manage to visit the Chateau de Versailles, the Eiffel Tower, and the Orsay Museum, but by the third day we're anxious to get to Istanbul.

We hadn't realized how exhausting train trips can be until we were finally on one. After a nine-hour journey to Munich, we board yet another train operated by the Hungarian Train Company that will take us to Keleti Station, in the heart of Budapest.

We arrive at our reserved cabin to discover we're sharing it with another couple. Oliver and Danielle are students studying History at Cambridge and working together on a book about the last days of the Ottoman Empire. Since this is their third trip to Istanbul, they turn out to be knowledgeable and beneficial companions.

"Travelling up to Salzburg on the Austrian border will be in daylight," Oliver says, "but after that, there is nothing but darkness."

It's about 1:30 A.M. when the train grinds to a halt on the Hungarian border. We hear voices. Someone is shouting. A dog barks. Another dog responds. "That's border control," Oliver says. "They'll check our passports and visas, but what they're really looking for is cash. The Hungarian economy has been in the pits since the 1956 Uprising."

I feel sweat beads rolling down my back as I realize we don't have our visas. "Oliver, we were told we didn't need them. All we needed was to show our paid ticket stubs."

"Okay, let me handle this," Oliver suggests. "I've done it before."

At that moment there's a pounding on the door and an armed guard enters.

"*Passporte, passporte!*" he barks in a heavy accent. Another guard enters and peers over the shoulder of the first, watching as he flicks through the pages of each passport. The guard returns the three British passports, but retains and closely studies my chocolate-brown Kenyan passport. He lingers over the imprint of the shield, crossed spears and golden lions of the Kenyan coat of arms. He zeroes in on my photo again. In that suspended moment of silence, my blood pressure reaches outer space.

He says something in Hungarian to his colleague, who suddenly steps forward and hands me my passport and exits.

"Eighty Pounds," the guard says, in broken English, pointing to us in turn.

"If any of you have fivers (five British pounds) please give them to me," Oliver urges. "I need six of them."

Eleanor pulls out three five-pound notes and hands them to Oliver. Danielle also hands Oliver three five-pound notes. The guard is watching as Oliver counts out four of the fivers and hands them over. "These-are-for-visas. Four-people. Okay?"

He cautiously slips the remaining two five pound notes into the guard's breast pocket. "These-are-for- you-and-your-friend."

We hold our breath as we await a reaction to the blatant bribe.

"Okay. Goodbye." The Guard smirks and moves on to shakedown as many other passengers as he and his cohort can within the thirty-minute train stop.

"Wow. That was horrible Oliver, but thank you for dealing with it. It would never be permitted in Kenya," I affirm.

Oliver explains. "Five pounds is a lot of money in this economy. After years of post war survival, the Hungarian people were tired of their frugal lifestyle and showed it in 1956 when they revolted. It was a violent time.

"Listen, I noticed you have train tickets to Bucharest (Romania). Do you know that travelling there by train from Budapest will take you up to fifteen hours? Danielle and I are going to rest for a day in Budapest and then take an overnight bus via Belgrade that'll get us to Sofia, Bulgaria at about 9:30 A.M. The buses are really cheap in Sofia and so are accommodations. Very cheap. Why don't you join us?"

"Well, I'm all for it," Eleanor responds, clearly delighted. "I think I've had enough of sitting on trains for a while."

"Let's do it then," I agree.

"Wait…what if we can't get a refund?" she anxiously considers.

"I don't expect we will, but let's do it, anyway. I can't take another rendezvous with one more thieving guard."

Oliver and Danielle are experts on local food and wine and they also manage the language pretty well, which makes them choice travelling companions.

Sofia is a city founded over twenty-five hundred years ago. It's close to the foot of Vitosha Mountain which accounts for its comfortable climate and magnificent greenery. The architecture reflects the various cultures that occupied it at different stages. The main influence is classic Bulgarian and European, but throughout you can see a sprinkling of Orthodox churches with their distinctive domed roofs. When the Russians 'liberated' the Balkans from the declining Turkish Ottoman Empire in the mid-nineteenth century, sadly, they peppered the landscape with their style of heavy, drab, government buildings.

We are all seated at a café. "Please can we visit the Boyana church?" Eleanor pleads. "We have six hours before we have to get on the overnight train to Istanbul."

Within minutes we are on a tramcar headed towards the church. This proves to be a very worthwhile visit. The interior is covered with amazing frescoes that represent some of the best examples of Eastern medieval art over its twelve hundred year history.

Later, outside the church, we're trying to decide whether to take a taxi, or walk two blocks to the tramcar stop.

"Come with me," Oliver says, as he raises his hand and stops a minibus in its tracks without even a hint of the screeching of brakes. We get in. It's crowded, but very, very, cheap. The marshrutki, as minibuses are called, operate like Kenya matatus. They seem to ignore traffic rules, stopping wherever they like, diverting from fixed routes to bypass traffic congestion during rush hours. They're affordable and faster than other transit. I feel at home in Sofia.

At the end of a most interesting tour, we say our goodbyes to our new friends; and Eleanor and I board the overnight train to Istanbul.

Eleanor's excitement is palpable as we traverse the last few miles that deliver us into the sprawling metropolis of Istanbul. "Thank you luv." She squeezes my arm, as we gaze at the unfolding urban landscape. "It's always been my dream to come to Istanbul. So much of European history is tied to this city. Look, there it is! The Topkapi Palace! Please, Lando, once we check into our hotel, can we begin there?"

It's an easy decision. We were enamoured of Jules Dassin's 1964 film Topkapi with its wonderful story and magnificent setting.

"Look there, Eleanor, how the water separates in the shape of a horn? That's Cape Horn. There in the distance, is the Black Sea flowing through the Bosporus Straight into the Sea of Marmara."

We pull into the station at exactly 8:30 A.M. and take a taxi to our hotel. We check in and leave immediately to begin our tour of the Topkapi Museum that has us awestruck.

Through an English-speaking Turkish guide, we are infused with the history of Istanbul from the time it changed its name from Byzantium to Constantinople in 334 CE. We learn that's when it became the Christian capital of the Byzantine Empire. It had survived for more than a thousand years until the Ottoman Turks conquered it in 1453 CE and Sultan Mehmed renamed the city Istanbul. According to written records, he then ordered that the nearby Hagia Sophia Church be converted into a mosque.

We follow our guide as he enthuses over the design of the architecture, the interior embellishments, the geometric precision and colours of the structure and mosaic tiles. Unlike Christianity, Islamic places of worship do not permit images of the human form, so much is made of their exquisite use of perforated walls, light and shade, sculpture and carvings.

We walk through the palaces built around courts that are all cleverly linked together. Various sultans built additions between the fifteenth and nineteenth centuries. The Topkapi was the court of government for the life of the Ottoman Empire.

Four hours later, exhausted and overwhelmed, we sit in a

quiet corner of a café that is housed within the palace.

"What debauchery must have taken place over these centuries," Eleanor whispers. "I mean, six floors of space for a Harem of three hundred concubines and their black eunuchs? But I do love all those sumptuous gardens and lavish water-fountains."

"I couldn't get over the opulent pavilions designed for different types of gatherings. And what about the treasury with all the embossed jewels, gemstones, gold and silver?"

"Imagine how the few got away with living in such extravagant luxury, while their slaves, eunuchs, and general population starved outside the walls." Eleanor sighs.

"Come darling, let's go to the Hagia Sophia to see if the Christians did any better."

Byzantine architecture and art reflect a strong Christian influence. The large imposing dome and the frescoes covering the walls and ceilings with scenes from the scriptures, are impressive. There are abundant displays of sacred art and sculpture. There are paintings and miniatures, expertly crafted ornaments, and silver and gold embroidered vestments.

That evening we walk by the many fish restaurants that populate the lower level of the Galata Bridge, built in the nineteenth century. "I could live here forever," Eleanor says.

"We'll come back on holiday," I reply. "There's still so much to see."

We spend the next day, touring the Grand Bazaar and other examples of fine Ottoman mosque design like the Blue Mosque with its exquisite hand painted blue tiles throughout its interior, its six minarets and thirteen domes all intricately intertwined. It's one of the magnificent defining postcard silhouettes of Istanbul. Another is the Suleymaniye Imperial Mosque, built in the mid-sixteenth century. It is markedly different in its architecture. Its magnificent arched colonnade embraces a huge courtyard that surrounds exquisite gardens. The bulk of the buildings are grouped tightly together and demarcated by four minarets on the periphery.

Because my architectural training focused on Western European architecture, I hadn't imagined the scale, magnificence and sheer artistry that these examples of the Ottoman Empire represented. I feel architecturally saturated.

Over dinner, Eleanor and I discuss all the sights we had taken in that day.

"I can't get over the enormity of the Grand Bazaar," she enthuses.

"I know, and I can't get over the brass and copper utensils, Turkish kilims, silks, leather, mosaics, china, painted tiles and ceramics… thousands of items for sale."

"I've been reading about the Indian Bazaar in Nairobi, Lando? Is it anything like this?"

"Oh God, no. Not even if you could take all the stores in the Nairobi city centre and cluster them under one roof."

"So, there'll be no shopping for gold vestments when I arrive in Nairobi?" she teases with a giggle."

"No gold vestments, but we have beautiful African designs on kaftans if you're willing to sacrifice your sudden passion for gold embroidered religious robes."

"Ha, ha. I think I'll look just fine in a Kaftan, without the gold." She plants a kiss on my cheek as she rises from the table. "We should get some rest. I just realized that tomorrow will be our ninth day on the road."

"But hopefully it will be less hectic," I reply.

August 1, 1966

It's a short distance from the hotel to the car-ferry dock at Yenikapi on the Golden Horn. We arrive with just minutes to spare. The ferry takes about four and half hours to cross the Marmara Sea to the dock at Bandirma. We are lucky to find seats on the upper deck. It's such a relief to be out of the unremitting summer heat of Istanbul. I glance at Eleanor whose face is pink from the heat. I think how lovely she looks with the wind blowing through her sunlit hair. She squeezes my hand and smiles. "Thank you."

I return the smile. We are clearly happier than children on Christmas morning.

"It will be a six hour train ride to Izmir," I remind her. "So, let's keep our fingers crossed that we get to Pergamum tomorrow. We have confirmed tickets for the ship out of Izmir the day after, so we can't be late. There are no refunds and these are really expensive tickets."

It was Professor McCaughan at the University of Liverpool who enthusiastically claimed Pergamum as one of the best-recovered archaeological cities in the world. His slides and lectures persuaded us to include it on our trip.

The train ride is uneventful, so thankfully we arrive on time. We strike a deal with a taxi driver outside of our hotel for the next day's trip to Pergamum.

The city was first built in the fifth century BCE, but came into its own around thirty CE. It was eventually given to the Romans. During Grecian times, Pergamum boasted the biggest Library after Alexandria. Under Roman Rule, Mark Anthony gifted the collection of over two hundred thousand books to Queen Cleopatra of Egypt!

As we are standing at the top edge of a massive amphitheatre looking down into the arena thinking of gladiators and lions, Eleanor whispers, "Lando, I feel like I'm fading." I swiftly wrap my arms around her. She is indeed fading. The heat is unbearable. I help her to some nearby shade. Our taxi driver appears like magic with a cool bottle of water. Much to Eleanor's chagrin, he urges us to return to the hotel. She reluctantly agrees but insists she'll be up and ready to go in the morning.

The next day, she is up at the first hint of sunrise. The same taxi driver takes us to Cesme for a refreshing swim in the Aegean Sea which turns out to be a real treat. He suggests Eleanor and I take a short ferry ride to the Greek island of Chios for lunch before returning to our hotel in Izmir.

I'm at the other end of the ferryboat, when Eleanor calls out to me. She's talking to a gentleman who looks to me to be distinctively Turkish.

"I'm Antoniou Papadopoulos and I'm pleased to meet you." The man has a Greek name and introduces himself in perfect English. I realize, I couldn't have been more wrong as he continues. "Your wife tells me you are from Kenya. I was a dentist in Moshi, Tanganyika. My clinic was on the Old Moshi Road."

"Ah, good to meet you, Mr. Papadopoulos. Have you retired here?"

"Antoniou, please," he says. "Call me Antoniou. Yes, after the 1964 coup in Zanzibar…that is now part of Tanzania. They raped and killed so many people; Asian women, Arabs and Africans. My wife said, 'We will be next, you can stay if you must, but I'm going!' We closed the practice. Imagine that. I gave up everything after thirty-two years. I had no choice."

"I'm sorry to hear that. Have you opened a dental practice here?" I ask.

"No need to. I have a flat I rent to tourists. Food is cheap. *Retsina* is almost free."

"Sounds like heaven." I smile.

"No! It is hell. In heaven there are angels who talk to each other about beautiful, interesting things. Here, these people gossip about nothing all day. They have not been abroad. They don't even read papers. It is hell."

"Can you talk to tourists?" Eleanor asks.

"Am I not talking to you?" He chuckles. "Where are you eating lunch?" he asks.

"Can you recommend some place?" I'm hungry and thirsting for a beer.

"Yes, of course. Come with me." He recommends a restaurant and joins us as we all indulge in a delectable assortment of superb Greek foods.

Antoniou is pleased that we share his love for Africa and

excited to have someone he can have a real conversation with. I try to pay the bill for the three of us, but he graciously insists on treating us. We hug and say goodbye, promising to return to Chios one day soon.

"*Efharisto para poli*," (Thank you very much) Eleanor declares. She remembered the phrase from our taxi driver.

"*Asante, Kwaheri and Kuonana*," (Thank you, goodbye till we meet again) Antoniou replies in Swahili as he walks us to the ferry. I think I see his eyes tear up, but I definitely sense his loneliness in what seemed a paradise to us.

* *

The next day, we embark on a Greek ferryboat ride from Izmir to Piraeus, the Port for Athens. Our accommodations are sleeping bags on an open deck, under a million stars, all for four dollars a night. Not five-star luxury, but... there was a shower and toilet.

As soon as we arrive in Athens, we rush about visiting monuments, then decide to explore life in a couple of residential areas outside the tourist hot spots. We eat in small modest restaurants that serve wholesome food at cheap prices. Language proves to be a barrier with older folks, but younger people will try to converse, or more accurately, to ask how to get to '*Amrika*.' There's little interest however, in how to get to the UK or Kenya.

On day twelve, we embark on an island-hopping cruise ship in Piraeus, that takes us south on the Aegean Sea, then west through the Corinth Canal to Patras and into the Ionian Sea for a four-hour excursion to the Island of Corfu.

The next day we arrive in Dubrovnik (Yugoslavia) at dawn for another short excursion, and then head across the Adriatic Sea to the port of Bari on Italy's East Coast.

As the landing ramp is being lowered onto the dock, Eleanor shares a gnawing concern. "Lando, I have a feeling we're running out of days. When we get to Rome tonight, we should seriously rethink our itinerary."

"You're right. I miscalculated how much time we would need in Asia Minor and even earlier, crossing Eastern Europe."

We catch the next train to Rome, zoom through various Italian cities, and make it to Paris, and Calais for our final cross-channel ferry that has us arriving back in England on the twenty-fourth of August.

12

A Short Trip… But a Long Journey

September 3, 1966

Departing Heathrow Airport, London.

The plane has reached its cruising level, the cabin lights are on, and the *Fasten Seat Belt* sign has turned green. The crew begins scurrying about performing their duties. In eight hours I'll be back in Nairobi, exhausted and desperately missing Eleanor.

Our 'European Safari,' as we now call it, was wonderful. We both learned so much about the powerful Empires that had once roamed, ravaged, conquered, and ruled vast areas of East Europe. We discovered how in each case, years of conflict and peace had left scars and cultural evidence in architecture, the arts, music and food.

Isolated Egyptian obelisks in Turkey, ancient Greek temple ruins, Roman baths and viaducts and Byzantine churches… monuments and more monuments to religious conquest. Mosques and mausoleums interspersed with Christian churches and palaces, adorned with works of art, patronized by the wealthy barons of the day to pay homage to the God that they believed helped them vanquish their enemies abroad, and at home, to amass their wealth on the backs of the poor.

Eleanor and I learned more about each other. I certainly realized how much fun it was to be with her.

* *

With nothing to distract me, besides the monotonous drone of the engines flying at about 33,000 feet, my thoughts begin to drift.

In the past week, Eleanor had coveted my rich red-brown leather suitcase that I had travelled with from Kenya. She insisted that we not leave it behind in England.

I smile as I recall the moment I acquired that suitcase at an auction only seven months before leaving Kenya, when I had neither a need for one, nor any travel plans. The auctioneer had started the bidding: *'Item #25. Beautiful antique leather case… fifty shillings, fifty, do I have fifty?'*

My hand shot up impulsively just as the hammer came down. There were no other bids. I proudly took my prize back to Plums Lane.

When I left Kenya in July of 1964, the suitcase was perfect for my travels to England. Now it's going back to Africa tightly packed with Eleanor's collection of 33 and 45-rpm vinyl records, along with another case I purchased to fill with more books and gifts for family. Hopefully both cases will arrive with me.

Have you ever stopped to look at a suitcase plastered with exotic labels and wonder what tales it would tell if it could speak? What story would my case tell? Did it carry the riches of some famous celebrity? Or the secrets of an infamous white settler who arrived by steamship, with only personal effects and a rifle? Perhaps it belonged to an adventurous woman who was seduced by the exotic tales of Elspeth Huxley or Karen Blixen and was escaping the monotony of British society?

I wonder if Eleanor might now see herself as Huxley or Blixen.

I recall my father Chico's story about his black tin trunk which my uncle had purchased at a store near Bombay's famous Victoria Station. It had begun its original journey in Wolverhampton, England, in 1924. Was it coincidence or a karmic occurrence that Eleanor too should embark on her journey from Wolverhampton?

My uncle had intended to take the trunk with him to Africa and from there to Brazil; but instead he gifted it to my dad in Goa. Four years later in 1928, Dad brought it to Kenya and since then, it made three return sea voyages to India.

I remember in 1949 watching as Chico emptied its contents of mementos and memories and spoke of family I had never heard of. I was only ten then and was about to embark on a voyage of my own across the Indian Ocean, bound for a Jesuit boarding school in Goa.

"Lando, you must be its next owner," Dad had declared.

"Thank you Dad... I will keep it forever." Over the next few days, I had re-filled it with a few of my own belongings and numerous gifts from my parents to give to distant strangers I had never met.

Two years later Anja, my dearest mother, was distraught when I declared my wish to join the priesthood and a fervent desire to transfer into a nearby seminary immediately. I was quickly whisked back to Kenya with trunk in tow.

After forty years of faithful service, it was transformed into a piece of furniture in my room, simply by draping it with a faded kilim (a tightly woven cotton rug) and a couple of brightly coloured cushions that give no clue to the fresh load of worthless sentimental junk that now fills its belly. I wonder what Eleanor will think of my 'Garage Abode' when she arrives in Kenya?

I doze off to sleep.

* *

I've arrived and so has my luggage.

Whiskey is delirious! He barked incessantly for about an hour after my arrival. Mum says he couldn't adjust to my leaving for the UK, and he kept sniffing under the front door for weeks hoping I might have returned while he was asleep.

Mum and Dad have heard all about Eleanor and our plans for the future from me, and then from Uncle Renato and then Linda who had both written glowing reports about her. So my parents are now looking forward to welcoming her to Nairobi and the family. Mum is relieved that there will be time to prepare for the wedding. She bombards me with questions about Eleanor's tolerance for Goan cooking, her familiarity with Indian spices, her culinary skills and willingness to be trained. I discretely deflect those questions, but am comfortable in my opinion that they will love each other, and she should not become anxious over Eleanor.

Dad is concerned about my finding a job and housing before Eleanor joins me. He slips in a little homily about marriage and the responsibilities it entails, and the challenges of marrying outside the community.

"*Amorsino*," Mum interrupts him. "They are young. They must find out for themselves what life is about. There will be many ups and downs, even real disagreements between them. Have you forgotten how we started our married life?"

Mum turns to me "Will my grandchildren, your children, be brought up Roman Catholic? Have you discussed this with Eleanor and a priest in Liverpool?"

"Yes Mum, we will be meeting with a priest before the wedding. There's still time to arrange those things."

"What news of Stephen?" I ask. So far no one had mentioned his name.

"He hasn't been around for a long while. I really don't know how he manages to survive. It must be difficult as he needs to support his mother and sister," Dad says. "But he will somehow hear of your return via the 'bush telegraph' and will turn up now that you're here, just you wait and see."

I move back into my converted garage, which has been lovingly prepared for my arrival. Whiskey takes up his spot outside my door signaling his '*till death do us part*' devotion.

Monday morning, I embark on my job search. I'm almost sure a job at Nairobi City Hall awaits me. After all, the Government had selected me for a scholarship.

I make an appointment to see Kevin Craig-McFeely, the

Chief Planner. His kind blue eyes twinkle behind wire-rimmed bifocals, as he welcomes me into his office. He describes the challenges Nairobi is facing with the explosive urban migration since Independence. I feel comfortable talking about my specific interest in changing the profile of housing in the African areas, and in helping to modify the official approach to low-income housing.

He tells me that he will be retiring in a couple of years and as the challenges are immense, he must train his successors. "Trust and integrity will be a paramount requirement. The political pressures to bend the rules have already started."

"Where would I fit in?" I ask.

"The policy is to have a qualified African in my job. We already have a good man Gilbert Njau. He was appointed while you were in England, so you will not have met him yet. You will both do very well together. You, as an Asian Kenyan, could be his deputy… in other words, the number two position. We have two other graduates who will be arriving after attending City Planning courses in the USA."

Kevin tells me that all salary grades have been restructured to bring more parity to local government salaries. Prior to independence, salary grades were structured by race. He asks about my marital status. I tell him about Eleanor, and our future plans. He asks whether I've checked on the market rates for rental housing as these have escalated tremendously during my absence. He explains that as a Kenyan national, there would be a cap on my salary, and if I choose to live in a previously European designated area, it might not cover my rent.

I'm in a quandary. I need a job and the city is the best option for what I want to do in the area of low cost housing. On the other hand, I can't bring Eleanor to Kenya and expect her to live a precarious existence. Kevin seems to read my thoughts.

"Why don't you try the Department of Regional Planning in the Lands Office," he says. "Central government pays much higher salaries than Local Government."

As I 'm on my way out of City Hall, I notice David Cook, the Deputy City Engineer, walking back to his office. I approach and he seems sincerely happy to see me.

"We've been awaiting your return from Liverpool," he says. "I love Liverpool. My wife was born there. They used to joke that the best thing about that place was the train to London. So when do you start?"

"Sadly I had to turn down an offer in the Planning Department, as the mandated pay scales for Kenyan nationals does not even cover the cost of a market-priced small apartment in the Delamere Flats."

He seems shocked and invites me to step into his office. He tells me he has embarked on a personal mission to transform the collective mindset of young engineers, planners and architects. "Imagine if everyone understood their respective contribution to urban development and shaping the city as part of a comprehensive plan. I intend to bring the technical people on city staff together with their local counterparts in the private sector, and expatriate consultants, to discuss urban issues and stimulate fresh thinking. Whatever you end up doing, I'm inviting you now. Good luck in the job hunt."

That evening, I'm feeling despondent over the interview at City Hall but I don't want to create anxiety at dinner with the family. Whiskey senses something is wrong and takes to following me around for the next two days. Dogs are amazingly intuitive companions who always seem to know when your morale is low.

Two days later, I have an interview with Sidney Lock, Chief Regional Planner and long-time Kenya resident who seems pleased to see me.

"I met your old boss Graham McCullough at Muthaiga (Country Club) last night and we happened to talk about you. He knows you're back and needs you in his office," he says. "The private sector pays so much better. Sure, here we pay a bit more than City Hall, but Government can't compete with private practice. You'll be better off there. Shame really, old boy, but that's the way the official government salaries have been set up."

I'm taken aback by his honesty. I know he's genuine and looking out for what's best for me. We discuss the pace of urbanization in smaller towns that are exploding in growth. Land use planners are in great demand. Engineers are also in desperate short supply. After the interview, I'm left to wonder how Government will work in the future if everyone is earning 'African' salaries but aspiring to higher living standards. Was that not in part what the fight for Uhuru was about? Will Kenya go the way of India with its miserable public salaries that force everyone to seek additional compensation through bribes and baksheesh?

I'm walking back towards City Hall, when I hear my name, "Lando, I didn't know you were back!" It's Stewart Wallace, Basil's friend who met me at the airport in 1964 as I was leaving for the UK. I recall the thick sealed envelope he handed me from Basil, which I mailed for him in England.

"Just back," I say. We pop into a coffee shop. He tells me that Basil and family managed to get out safely and he doesn't expect him to return anytime soon. I'm curious.

"There's a lot of '*maneno*' (gossip) about nefarious goings on," he says, adding ominously, "Better for you not to know these things."

* *

Within a week, I'm back at work with my old employer, Graham McCullough.

* *

Two airmail letters arrive from Eleanor. She's missing me as much as I'm missing her. Soon there's a beautiful deluge of correspondence to and from the UK. Whiskey makes it a point of accompanying me every evening as I read excerpts aloud. Eleanor always sends him love too, and I swear he cocks his ears to listen for it.

In the weeks that follow, we each average at least two letters a week. Eleanor is seeking answers on my job prospects, house search, and so forth. She also describes the latest twists and turns of life in the UK. She entertains me with backroom gossip from family and friends about her rash decision to gamble her life in a foreign land, known to be infested by Mau-Mau terrorists, wild animals, gigantic mosquitos, yellow fever, malaria, bilharzia and the dreaded tsetse fly.

For me the weeks seem long but the work is interesting. Weekends are the worst. Many of my contemporaries seem to have re-grouped socially. We all attended the Dr. Ribeiro Goan School, but our Goan clubs of our parents' generation divided us by 'class'. We now meet on neutral ground. The most popular of which is Brunner's Snooker Parlour in the Queens Hotel, near City Hall. It was one of the first to open up to all races once the segregation laws were removed. Cyprian Fernandes, who we know as 'Skip' is the uncrowned 'king' here. He's one of our own, who started from humble beginnings, and is now one of the most popular Sports Reporters with the Nation Group. Though he writes well, he is better at telling good yarns when not constrained by the rigors of journalism. I find his stories and the innuendos and subterfuge of post-independence Kenyan politics, both informative and unnerving.

I look for my High School colleagues who I discover went abroad to study and never came back. Of the University batch, it's a similar story. Of the three or so that are still around, they too have started the application process to emigrate for a better future. I'm beginning to feel nervous about whether Eleanor and I are making the right move; but I must not worry her.

I respond to Eleanor's letters. I explain I'm stuck in a mundane role in Nairobi, earning money, finding us accommodation in a tight rental market, and restoring social contacts after a two-year absence when many friends and colleagues have quietly slipped away to the UK, Canada, Australia and New Zealand.

It's so good to come home daily to a doggie hug from Whiskey.

13

An Arranged Marriage

Ours is an arranged marriage. Eleanor and friends have arranged every detail from the guest list to my rented morning suit and hat.

I receive a note confirming that a Church has been booked for January 5, 1967. A letter from Eleanor arrives with a questionnaire from 'Moss Bros.' the renowned Men's Bespoke Outfitters. They require every measurement imaginable, and unimaginable, for my suit and hat rental.

I also receive a notification that a Catholic priest who has agreed to perform the ceremony, will not insist on Eleanor's conversion to Catholicism; 'providing:

1. Both parties attend religious instruction together for three days before the marriage ceremony; and

2. Both parties commit, in an oral agreement, that any children they will have, consequential to the union, will be baptized into the Catholic faith.'

What comforts me most is Eleanor's response: "My darling Lando, we have a deal."

* *

About four months earlier, on July 18, 1966, my first cousin from Mozambique had turned up in Liverpool. We had never met before. He had arrived with supporters of the Portuguese soccer team, who had already played two winning games at Trafford Stadium Manchester, in the FIFA World Cup Soccer Tournament in England. Tiny Portugal was to play the legendary soccer giant Brazil, the next day at Goodison Park Liverpool.

Over dinner, he insisted that Eleanor and I visit Portugal for our honeymoon and meet the rest of the family. I expressed doubts about being able to get a visa as I travel on a Kenyan passport, but he confidently allayed my concerns.

"Lando, Cascais is home to all the deposed and exiled royalty of Europe, as well as other self-exiled dignitaries, shady businessmen and erstwhile politicians from other countries. The world-famous Casino in Estoril was built specifically to help these ageing cohorts recover from the shock of being deposed and help them fade away gracefully." He takes a sip of wine, and continues, "And one more thing my dear *Primo* (cousin), what's most important for you to know is that I'm the Chief Architect and Planner for the City of Cascais, for God's sake. So, just present my letter and doors will open for you."

We were convinced. We will go to Portugal for our honeymoon.

* *

About ten days before the Christmas of '66, and three weeks before the wedding, I arrive in England to help with any last minute arrangements… and to obtain the necessary visas for our planned honeymoon in Portugal.

I had assembled all the possible documents, forms, photographs and affidavits that we were likely to need. Eleanor and I take the train to Euston in London and connect with the Tube to the Portuguese Consulate.

A plain-clothes, English-speaking security guard, stops us at the entrance and demands to see our passports. He looks at Eleanor's British passport and hands it back without comment. Then he glances at me, then at my Kenyan passport and hands it back as if it were contaminated.

"No!" He declares. His body language implies he is willing to lay down his life to defend his decision. His words are clear. "The Republic of Portugal does not maintain diplomatic relations with Kenya. We cannot issue you a visa." I show him the letter from my Portuguese cousin. Since it is directed to: 'To Whom it May Concern,' I assume that means President Antonio Salazar himself. According to my cousin's assurances, this letter 'would open doors.' The security officer repeats: "We do not maintain relations with Kenya nor with any Independent black African country! And we don't intend to start now. Goodbye!"

And with that, he slams the door on us, and on our dreams of a Portuguese honeymoon. "What now? What are we going to do?" Eleanor is understandably upset.

"My darling, if you're going to live in Kenya, you must learn to think on your feet," I cheerfully reply. But in my own inner panicked state, I'm desperately looking for inspiration to guide us, or my feet, to hurry us away from this dilemma.

Suddenly, there it is… staring us in the face. A black, white and green striped flag, a crimson triangle superimposed with a seven-pointed white star, fluttering right next door to the Consulate.

"Eleanor, my boss has given me time off until January 15th, so let's go to Jordan and say hello to our old classmate Shukri and his family." We both promised to come one day. They'd be delighted. It'll be nice to visit the ancient city of Petra after hearing so much about it from Professor McCaughan. Oh, and we can visit the Holy Land too. Think of it, darling, Bethlehem, Jerusalem and Jericho. We can even head home via Cairo.

Eleanor's smile and embrace is all the confirmation I need.

"Okay, agreed!" Within forty-five minutes we're walking away with visas for our trip to the Hashemite Kingdom of Jordan.

* *

Back in Wolverhampton, preparations for the wedding are going well until Eleanor gets a message from her mother, which simply says; *'Lando has an enormous head.'* I feel the hair on the back of my neck begin to bristle. Fortunately the issue was quickly resolved. There was an error in the Moss Bros. rental company questionnaire that I had filled in from Nairobi. It seems that there was a problem converting inches to centimetres, thus making my head the size of a giant.

* *

On our wedding day, my best man, Nigel, and I are travelling to the church together. We're both strangers to the city but since he's a non-driver, I'm designated, although I have barely driven a total of five days on British roads. We study the map, plot our route, Nigel will navigate, and off we go in the direction of the church.

Within a few of miles of our destination, Nigel suggests a quick shot of whiskey will calm his nerves, so we pull up at the first pub we come across and then waste precious minutes waiting for it to open.

After being *spiritually* reinforced, I carefully exit onto the main road. "Sh*t!" Nigel shouts as he points to a construction roadblock. We reroute… and within minutes we're lost. Completely lost. We've been sucked into a horrendous labyrinth of one-way signs and temporary diversions. We pull the car onto a parking lot to take stock.

"I estimate, we're likely about three miles from the church, as the crow flies," Nigel declares. I instinctively look around and remember I am not in my motherland, Goa, where crows abound, squawk the day's gossip from dawn to dusk, and fly about erratically.

Thankfully, a kindly old gentleman walking his dog helps us with proper directions and a shortcut.

There's a collective gasp from the guests as Nigel and I step inside the church. We've arrived a few minutes late and slightly unnerved, only to discover that Eleanor and her entourage led by her dearest friend and now Bridesmaid, Judith, are also going to be late.

Once the bride and groom finally take their places, the ceremony is beautiful. The reception in a nearby hotel is wonderfully well organized. The anxiety that we caused our guests by arriving late, seems to drive everyone to drink to excess. The Emcee keeps the speeches from the line-up of inebriated guests from going awry. Eleanor's parents are gracious hosts. It's an exquisite reception...but unfortunately, Eleanor and I are too excited and overwhelmed to remember much of anything.

* *

The trip to Jordan is highlighted by our visit to the ancient city of Petra; once prosperous, later abandoned and recently rediscovered. The driver, Omar, who takes us there from Amman, makes periodic stops on route where we are offered tea and snacks. Eleanor and I partake but nothing touches his lips. It is January, the month of Ramadan, and Omar explains to us that he must fast until sunset.

In the port city of Aqaba, Omar tells us that Aqaba, Jordan is a journey of less than three kilometres to Eilat, Israel. Both resort cities sit at the head of the Red Sea. He takes us to a lookout point. "Israel is right over there," he says as he points. "We are only 10 minutes, but hundreds of years apart." I don't quite understand the issue. I admit to being ignorant of the politics of this entire region. The only places that are familiar to me are biblical names like Jerusalem, Jericho and Bethlehem. Eleanor says it has something to do with the Arabs being upset over the British Mandate that divided the land. She remembers her father saying that at one time, he was to be drafted to keep the peace in Palestine, but his tour was cancelled.

Our itinerary is tight. We rush to devour the sights and ingest the flavours while we unfortunately also inhale miles of dust. Having only ten days of sanctioned leave from work, we can't waste a moment, so we brush off the dust and move on.

We visit Jerusalem during this important Muslim festival, one day before the fasting period ends. Sweet stores and butcher's shops line the Sacred Way of the Cross (Via Dolorosa). Freshly slaughtered goats with their heads intact, hang from beams. Their staring eyes make us wonder if they were taken by surprise.

We visit Jericho, the Dead Sea and Bethlehem. At first glance, everything seems to be as it was in biblical times. But after two thousand years, and a closer look, some of those places are beginning to show signs of crass modernity.

We spend a fantastic day touring a booming and boisterous Beirut, Lebanon. We return after dinner and dance the evening away at the nightclub in our hotel.

* *

We rise for an early breakfast before heading for the airport en route to Nairobi. Lingering over coffee, we share our favourite honeymoon moments and talk about our future.

"I absolutely loved the desert landscape on the drive down to Aquaba. The colours of the hills and valleys of sand, the camel caravans… it was straight out of Lawrence of Arabia," I wistfully recall.

"Lando, wasn't it wonderful to dance all night? Promise me we can come back to Beirut." She tenderly kisses my cheek and I pull her ever closer to me and whisper: "That's an easy promise to make, my darling. It's the only place in all our travels that inspired us to dance all night. We have to come back."

"I can't believe we're finally married and on our way to Kenya. It's like a fairy tale," Eleanor gleefully muses.

14

Kenya, Here We Come

The arrival lounge at Cairo Airport is a dizzying chamber of sounds and smells. Our flight from Beirut has arrived late and we are now destined to wait among a throng of other unhappy travelers. A thick, prolonged fog in London caused an indefinite postponement of our connecting flight to Nairobi. Two hapless airline attendants are bombarded with questions amid the intrusion of booming PA announcements, the babble of Arabic and South Asian dialects, loud demands in German, French and Italian, and a brash American leading a tour group of irate tourists.

In the overheated and tightly packed waiting room; hair spray, French perfumes, deodorants, cigarettes and sweat, swirl together to create a toxic brew. Everyone is either simmering with anxiety, nausea or anger, but somehow Eleanor remains calm. I smile as I grasp that this is the reward of being a cool headed Brit.

"Welcome to Africa, my darling… stifling as it may be at this moment, Egypt is your first step onto African soil." I whisper as I give my bride a reassuring hug. I wonder if she realizes what I've always known… that once you live in Africa, you can never live anywhere else again. It changes you forever.

"Well, Lando, the truth is, I've dreamed of visiting the pyramids… but this suffocating room isn't that… over there," she says, pointing to a compelling poster of Giza. "Maybe we should have planned to stay here a couple of days so we could see it."

A man standing next to us asks. "Would you like to go and see it? We could share the cost of a taxi?" I look at him as if he's quite mad. "Sorry, let me explain. I am Klaus and this is my wife, Angelika. We are Lutheran missionaries going to Arusha in Tanganyika… I mean, Tanzania," he corrects himself. "We are waiting for our flight, as are you. So we're going to take a quick trip to see the pyramids of Giza."

"Uh, I'm Lando and this is my wife, Eleanor." We shake hands. "We're on the same plane but we're flying to Nairobi. I like your idea, but do we have time?"

"Yes, Yes," Klaus assures us. "We have five hours. We need less than three. This man, Abdel, I have spoken to, will take us in his taxi."

The taxi driver introduces himself: "Call me Abdel, but please do not call me Nasser, or someone might kill me." He chuckles at his own joke but then feels he must explain it to the foreigners. "Gamal Abdel Nasser, led the coup in 1952 that overthrew King Farouk, and now he's the President of Egypt. Not everyone is a fan."

We exit the airport and step into the blazing sun. Within minutes, we are embarked on a daredevil ride through Cairo's chaotic streets. Donkey-pulled carts, bicycles, and motor cycles; lorries, cars, and utility vehicles compete for road space. The cars try to outperform each other with their horns. A lone, decorated camel is trudging towards Giza, its handler bearing the abuse from angry motorists. Pedestrians spill out from packed narrow sidewalks onto the roads, and frantically try to climb back again.

Within forty minutes we are standing awestruck at the foot of the Pyramids of Giza. It's a magnificent sight as the clean geometric lines and beautiful proportions stand in stark contrast against a clear azure sky. The oldest, tallest and best preserved is that of Pharaoh Khufu. His son, Pharaoh Khafre, built the second, to which he added the Great Sphinx to guard over his tomb.

The ancient Pharaohs unknowingly created Egypt's modern economy which is so reliant on international tourism, of which Giza is the starting point. The flat plateau at the base of the pyramids is teaming with tourists delivered by buses and taxis. Handlers dressed in *keffiyahs* (cloth headdress) and *kaftans*, wait by their camels and horses to make a sale. They are an assortment of hustlers, touts, and curio-vendors, offering paintings on sheets of papyrus, and 'antiquities' in alabaster and bronze, silver, gold and marble. Itinerant vendors sell 'genuine' identical copies of necklaces, brooches, bangles and rings that once adorned the great queens of Egypt.

Abdel has carefully locked up his taxi and is now our guide. He studied history and antiquities at Cairo University but opted to be self-employed as do thousands of like graduates each year.

He tells us to keep a scarf handy, in case of a sudden dust storm. We follow him until he stops and lights a cigarette. "This area is the best for photos." Klaus and Angelika amble one away while Eleanor and I are drawn in a different direction toward the Sphinx.

Handlers in white kaftans stand by their kneeling camels. The animals are adorned with brightly coloured saddle rugs and wait patiently while their masters scan potential clients for their photo business.

Eleanor looks at me, signaling she would like a photo for our honeymoon album. I signal back, okay, but at that same moment, I'm fixated on the sun's rays glimmering on the mouth of the Sphinx. I call out: "Sure, darling, let's do it, but I just have to snap that Sphinx's smile first." She nods her approval.

Barely two minutes later, there's a commotion.

"Lando, help, Lando!" I turn to see Eleanor mounted precariously on the camel that is now rising from its kneeling position. She's clinging to the stub handle of the saddle and all her typical British cool has evaporated. "Let me down, you…" She is red-faced and spewing whatever anger she can muster at the hustler. Abdel comes running to the rescue, shouting words in Arabic. We arrive at the camel together. The handler tightens the reigns to restrain the animal. I stand next to it, trying to figure out how to get her down. My head only reaches to Eleanor's knees. I turn to seek help when Abdel suddenly snaps a photo, which prompts the camel to casually return to a kneeling position whereby I step up to *rescue*

Eleanor.

"I'm sorry, I panicked," she giggles. "I've read so many stories about Sheikhs kidnapping blue-eyed blondes for their desert harems."

"Sorry, no desert harem for you," I chuckle. "I kidnapped you first." It was somehow refreshing to see her lose her British calm… even for an instant.

On the way back to the airport, Abdel promises to send us the photo of our first encounter with a camel. He then tantalizes us with highlights of Cairo we will only have time to see when we return.

"Everyone always comes back to Egypt," he says with confidence.

Klaus asks him what he knows about the Coptic Christian community. Abdel tells us about the 'Zabbaleen' (Arabic for garbage people) living in a large slum in *Manshiyat Naser*, near the quarries where in ancient times they likely chipped away the gigantic blocks of limestone for the pyramids. In a Muslim dominated society, the Coptics are a Christian community that has been relegated to collecting, sorting and recycling what can be salvaged of household waste from the city. After the pigs have foraged through the garbage, then Christian women and young girls are allowed to separate paper, plastics, and glass for resale.

As Eleanor and I are planners, we ask Abdel about Cairo's appalling housing overpopulation. He informs us that almost two hundred thousand people live in Cairo's City of the Dead, which is an ancient Islamic cemetery. It was once restricted to the graves and mausoleums of wealthy families who in turn constructed accommodations for their personal security guards. With the massive housing shortages in the city, the poor invaded this giant graveyard and now, Abdel tells us there are more living than dead residing in that cemetery.

Back at the airport, the four of us bid farewell to Abdel and then settle down in the waiting area amidst the nauseating sensory stew, to anticipate our flight. Exhausted from the heat, Eleanor leans her head on my shoulder and falls asleep.

* *

Our flight is announced. I gently nudge her awake.

"Darling, I'm getting really nervous about meeting your folks and friends," Eleanor whispers. "I've been thinking about what your mother said to you about not returning home with an English girl."

"Ah, my dear, you're forgetting the '*leaving the diploma behind*' part of her concern. That's the more worrisome scenario for my parents; and that I did not do. I'm bringing my urban planning degree as promised… and the girl of my dreams."

"But Lando, often when an outsider is brought into a small community, tensions are aroused in those mothers who have one less marriageable candidate available for their sons. I'm the outsider and I'm dreading meeting your ex-girlfriends and their mothers."

I laugh. "I don't think anybody's waiting in line. You've studied too much sociology, luv. You've heard the saying, 'In practice, the theory is always different?' They'll love you, you'll see."

We're aboard a BOAC flight from Cairo to Nairobi. Eleanor's warm, tousled head snuggles closer as she pulls the blanket tightly around her. I plant a kiss on her forehead and adjust to a more comfortable position. I shut my eyes, desperately hoping to catch a couple of hours of sleep. It's not the twisting in her seat and the snuggling closer that keeps me awake. It's worrying about the rushed details I sent to various contacts to make sure our apartment was ready for Eleanor's arrival. My high school mate, Mengha Singh, swore to me that our specially designed bed, with its beautiful dark-grained Meru oak headboard would be ready and delivered before my return. I must begin to trust that things will go as planned. I must remember, he promised. I breathe deeply and doze off.

I'm awakened by a buzz of activity near the flight kitchen. I look over at Eleanor. Her blonde highlights glow as a wisp of daylight peeks around the window shade. The cabin lights turn on and the stewardess announces that a light breakfast will be served prior to our landing in Nairobi. The Pilot's breezy voice takes over. He greets passengers and informs us that "We have just flown over Addis Ababa in Ethiopia and will soon be entering Somalian and Kenyan airspace. We will land at Jomo Kenyatta International Airport in Nairobi in ninety minutes. The temperature on the ground is heavenly." How does he know, I wonder?

Eleanor is suddenly struck again with a concern. "How will I manage without speaking Kiswahili? I don't want to let you down."

"My darling, everyone speaks English. And you already

know more Kiswahili phrases than most new arrivals. You may need to add some spicy kitchen vocabulary if we employ domestic servants, or eventually, an ayah to look after a baby, but that's years away."

As breakfast finishes, there's a traffic jam to get to the washrooms. Anticipation grows as we prepare for landing. We settle down, seat belts fastened, seat backs upright, and trays lifted and locked. Finally all is calm.

I raise the blind. Our BOAC Comet is making a slow descent as it skirts around the Ngong Hills. We are now on the final approach for landing on the Athi Plains. "Wow, Eleanor, look at that view." A brilliant, almost cloudless sky stretches into the horizon; the land is colour-washed in hues of purple, green and blue. Rays of red and orange stream from the rising African sun. In the distance, across the border in Tanzania, clusters of clouds hover over the crisp snow-covered, sun-drenched cone of Mount Kilimanjaro.

We have landed. We say goodbye to Klaus and Angelika, who must go into the transit lounge for their connection to Arusha, Tanzania.

* *

Mum and Dad, and a crowd of close friends are waiting to welcome us; and curious to see and meet Eleanor. As I watch them graciously welcome her, I feel privileged to have such friends in a community that always welcomes strangers. Eleanor's anxieties melt away as she is warmly embraced by all.

Ahmad is excited to be there to pick us up in his Chevy.

Driving away from the airport, I point out the Nairobi National Park to Eleanor.

"Oh gosh! It's almost in the city. Look, Lando, isn't that a giraffe?" Eleanor is astounded. She squeezes my arm and whispers, "I'm so thrilled to be here."

Dad points out new buildings that have gone up since my departure. Ever since I entered architectural school, he has become more interested in buildings and how they are changing the city's skyline. I notice a proliferation of billboards advertising products from around the world. It seems the previous restrictions imposed during colonial times, intended to protect British exports to Kenya, have been lifted.

"That's the stadium where the British flag finally came down at Independence," I proudly proclaim.

"They've changed a lot of the street names," Dad says. It will take you some time to figure out the new road signs." I detect a new enthusiasm in Dad's voice. Is it relief over my return? He must have felt tremendous anxiety while I was gone, watching so many of his friends leaving Kenya, never to return.

"See there? That's where all the 'big men' sit now," Mum sarcastically adds. "That's our Parliament building."

Eleanor is mesmerized by the trees and flowering shrubs along the highway. "How beautiful! I've never seen so much bougainvillea blooming at the same time and in so many different colours." She squeezes my hand and sighs, "I'm so happy to be here with you."

"Me too," I return her squeeze. "This is your new adopted

home. Our home … forever." Mum is looking out the window and smiling and no doubt thinking there's no chance now of Eleanor returning to England and taking me with her.

We arrive at Plums Lane, where Ahmad transfers our luggage directly into my VW Beetle. Whiskey introduces himself to Eleanor. He seems to instinctively know that displaying unconditional love for her will pay-off in the long term. Anyway, she smells good and has a kind face and seems to know exactly where to rub his neck.

Eleanor and I freshen up. A shower and clean clothes make such a difference.

After a tasty lunch, Mum launches into a quiz directed at Eleanor. It's interspersed with loving comments of 'how happy she is to have her as a part of the family' and of course, 'it will be very easy for her to make friends as there are many English people still around.' She suddenly begins to list statistics: "We Catholics love large families and my dream is to have at least twenty-five grandchildren from my six children. So Eleanor, how many children do you plan to have?"

Before Eleanor can conjure up a random number, I jump in and deflect. "Mum, Eleanor is really tired from the trip. And remember, she's here to stay forever, so there'll be lots of time for questions. Now I'm going to take her to our new apartment to rest up. We'll be back tomorrow to meet the rest of the family, which reminds me; when is Fatima expecting her third baby? And is there any news from Joachim in America?" Mum smiles as the message registers. "I'll give you all the news tomorrow. Now go home and get some rest."

We say our goodbyes, climb into my VW and head to our rental apartment, which is located in the famed Delamere Flats complex. It was renowned, prior to Independence, for the bright flamingo pink colour on the outside and 'whites only' policy on the inside.

"Are racial restrictions still in force?" Eleanor asks. I wonder if she's now realizing the implications of a mixed race union.

"Kenya has changed in many aspects, especially the colour bar which is officially gone forever," I reply.

We turn off Uhuru Highway onto what was previously Delamere Avenue and now renamed Kenyatta Avenue. I point out the Anglican Cathedral on our left.

"Tomorrow, we'll take a tour of the city and suburbs. There's so much I want to show you." I park the car in the carport. "First let's see your new home," I take her hand and lead her three floors up the curved stairway. I open the door. "Welcome home."

"I must sit down, Lando. Gosh, I'm feeling quite out of breath after only three flights. Do you know, in England, the Labour Government is still building six-story public housing walk-ups? I wonder how people can manage to get up and down all those stairs."

"Sorry luv, this is only a temporary place. We'll look for a proper house as soon as we're more settled." I don't tell her I'm paying 'European rent' on an Asian salary that barely covers it.

There is a beautiful bouquet of flowers on the tiny dining

table. "What lovely flowers." Eleanor picks up the card and reads: *Welcome Eleanor and Lando. With love, Chico and Anja.* Eleanor's salty tears slide down her cheeks and merge with mine as we join in a passionate kiss.

"Your Mum's so sweet, Lando," she says. "Do you know she wanted us to stay in your old garage studio for two weeks, so she could teach me Kiswahili and survival skills for Kenya, like where to shop for the best prices?"

"She'll still find a way to do that even if we don't live next door," I say. "My Mum was only seventeen when she arrived in 1935. She didn't speak a word of English or Kiswahili and she's often talked about the invaluable help she received from friends and neighbours; and because of that, she's always there to help other new arrivals."

"Oh, look! Mangos and bananas. We can only dream of these in England. They're so expensive there." Eleanor excitedly holds up a small woven basket with a card attached. "It's from your mother. It reads: *This is called a kikapu. Please keep it for your shopping.*

"Look here, the fridge is stocked. There's milk, butter, eggs, bacon, chipolatas, kippers and pickled herring. Here's a note. '*With compliments from Bishendas Bros at the Municipal Market.*' Do you eat pickled herring?" she asks.

"Not a chance, but Mum watches a lot of British TV reruns, and she's guessing that's what you English eat for breakfast. Come, darling, I have a surprise for you."

I lead her to our bedroom to show her the beautifully hand-crafted bed I had designed especially for her. What I find are two ugly metal folding cots. I'm about to explode; but taking a lesson from my cool-headed British wife, I instead, inhale deeply and explain.

"My darling, I designed a magnificent bed frame and headboard in Meru oak for us, and my friend promised to have it here and set in place before we arrived today, but obviously that has not happened. I'm furious… and so sorry."

She releases her enchanting giggle with abandon. "Oh luv, do you really think this is the only obstacle we'll ever have to overcome?"

I join in the humour of the moment with a few suggestions: "No my dear, this is Africa. Here there will be shortages, black market prices, exorbitant charges for simple imported goods, and delays on the delivery of items, like our bed for instance."

"*It's usually the simplest things that go wrong,* is a very British concept and a truism. So please don't worry, Lando. We'll push the cots together and it'll be fun… for now… just don't expect me to sleep on a camp cot forever."

"Oh don't worry about that, my luv, when I get through with my friend tomorrow, he'll get that bed here if he has to carry it on his back!"

15

Eleanor's New World

January in Kenya is unlike anywhere else on earth. Beautiful skies and perfect weather with daytime temperatures averaging about 26C and nights around 13C. Trees and flowers are in bloom. Birds broadcast their music from every tree. Even barking dogs in the suburbs are known to be less intrusive. Eleanor and I take a drive to explore the city centre. Earlier this week, she had glimpsed the large houses of the leafy suburbs with their immaculate lawns and beautiful gardens. We passed Muthaiga, Spring Valley, Lower Kabete, Langata and Karen, all once exclusively the domain of Europeans but now many name boards above the ubiquitous '*Mbwa Kali*' (savage dog) signs have African and Asian names.

Like any first-time visitor, the street landscaping enraptures her, especially along Kenyatta Avenue (Delamere Avenue) and Moi Avenue (Government Road). The margins and central reservation lined with flowering Flamboyant and Acacia trees. Jacaranda that missed their coming out party in late October, determined not to be forgotten, still display purple clumps on their branches. Gorgeous clusters of Bougainvillea in bright orange, crimson, white and magenta, interspersed with Hibiscus and other flowering shrubs dazzle in the sunlight. The roundabouts are landscaped with rock gardens adorned with giant 'candelabra' cacti and Estrelitzea (Natal Wild Banana), set in beds of varied other succulents.

"I hope one day I can introduce you to Peter Greensmith," I say. "He is one of the legends of this town. He came here as a young man after the War, found a job in the city and stayed. Rumour has it that he was given a free hand to beautify the city and within the space of three years, he had replanted all the main streets. Unfortunately, he had also blown the budget, including some of the money allocated to other parks and social services. But eventually, he was still regarded as a hero."

"He is *my* hero. I just love what he's done."

"He left City Hall just before Independence and opened a plant nursery and shop in Langata."

I turn right onto Moi Avenue, heading towards the Railway Station. With Eleanor's comments and questions as well as my exposure to urban planning, I find myself now seeing Nairobi through fresh eyes. The city centre is as clean and beautiful as I remember it prior to my departure for the UK. However, it has become visibly more crowded with pedestrians, and noisier with intense activity on the roads, especially by the *matatus*. The smell of diesel fumes permeates the dust. Not just more cars, but more brands abound. Prior to *Uhuru* almost all motor vehicles were predominantly British brands such as Ford, Morris, Austin, Bentley, and the ubiquitous Land Rover. There has been an obvious influx of new wealth everywhere and with it, new brands. Mercedes (most of them flying government or diplomatic flags), Volvos, Peugeots and Fiats imported from Europe seem to have overtaken the British imports. Even more conspicuous are Japanese brands like Toyotas, Nissans and Hondas. These cars pack the streets seeming to overwhelm in numbers, the bigger more expensive cars. Within this melee, matatus, lorries, zebra-striped safari vans and an assortment of pickup vans compete for space. In spite of this onslaught, the road surfaces in the city centre appear to still be in a good state of repair, after the facelift they received in preparation for the arrival of Uhuru in 1963.

On our return home after dark, we are astonished by the proliferation of new flashing neon signs announcing internationally recognizable brand names. These signs garishly announce that Kenya has emerged from the shadow of colonialism when, once imports from the rest of the world were restricted to those products manufactured in Britain, or selected member countries of the Commonwealth. Independence has opened Kenya to products and services of multinational corporations that owe allegiance to no country. No, they report to globally dispersed anonymous stock-holders.

It's a Saturday morning, Eleanor's second weekend in Nairobi, we stop by the Thorn Tree Café at the world-renowned New Stanley Hotel. It's buzzing with people, mostly tourists. Two young smartly dressed attractive black women walk past us and sit at an adjacent table. I can tell that they're the new generation of overseas-trained Kenyans, now back from the UK or the USA to serve our independent country.

Eleanor leans forward and says softly '*maridadi sana*' (very beautiful) referring to their sophisticated 'Masai-inspired' designer necklaces.

"Is one of those pretty girls, Saboti?" Eleanor smiles mischievously.

I had told her once about my infatuation with Saboti, but since she hadn't brought it up again, I assumed she'd forgotten about it. But I have heard tell that women will file away even inconsequential information, for instant retrieval when threatened.

"*Hapana*, it's not her. She's gone forever. Lives in the UK now."

She smiles and squeezes my hand.

A red-faced, sweating man in a safari hat and khaki shirt and shorts, accompanied by two 'well-weathered' European women, both with shoulder *kikapus* (bags) wander by, talking loudly.

I lean forward and whisper to Eleanor. "They're *Mzungus*,"

"It's so cosmopolitan in the city-centre," she says. "How can you tell who's who?"

"You don't need to tell the difference. They'll announce themselves."

"What do you mean?"

A waiter arrives, takes our order and leaves us alone. I embark on an overview for Eleanor. I explain that all Africans are called the *Wananchi* – sons of the soil. Within this group are different tribes, especially the Kikuyu, Luo, Masai, and Wakamba, to be seen around Nairobi. "And there are the

Samburu, the Turkana and the Karamajong from Northern Kenya."

Eleanor looks bewildered. "I had no idea."

"There are also the Taita and Swahili and other coastal tribes that you will meet when we go down to Mombasa. In time, you will be able to recognize them by their different features or dress." Our waiter arrives with our coffee and pastries.

A group of loud-talking German tourists file past, which is my cue to explain about the Europeans who collectively are called the *Wazungu* though individually a white person is called a *Mzungu*, pronounced '*Mu-zun-gu*'.

"And what about the different Europeans, beside the Brits?" Eleanor asks.

"Nobody bothers. There are only *mzuri* (good) *Mzungu*, and *mbaya* (bad) *Mzungu*," I say, "though I have heard that since independence there has been an influx of Europeans, Americans and Canadians who are not comfortable being called *Wazungu*, because of the colonial connotation. These folks are consultants or they represent foreign corporations."

"So what are they called?"

"I'm not sure. I've heard someone call them *Wageni* - that means 'guests' in Kiswahili - that's a new word for your vocabulary. '*Wa-geni*' makes sense as they are here in Kenya temporarily."

"What is word for 'I' in Kiswahili?"

"'I' is *Mimi*. 'You' is *Wewe*."

"So, *Mimi*, *Wageni*, yes?"

"Exactly! That is until you settle in and become truly Kenyan. Then you graduate and will be a Mzungu... you can then decide whether you want to be a good or a bad Mzungu."

"And what about your *kabila* (kind)? The Goans?"

"The Kenyans refer to brown people as *Wahindi*," I say. We are also labelled separately as Goans, Seychellois, Indians, Pakistanis, Lankan, or Mauritians but are collectively lumped into a basket marked 'Asians' by the Europeans. In practice, each community has its own clubs, as their respective religions have shaped their culture. It seems confusing when you first hear about the differences, but you will get to see this first hand." Eleanor smiles and looks around as if hoping to discover a 'species' I have not listed. We finish our coffee and leave our waiter happy.

"Okay. Come luv, we must be going. There's more to see."

Outside the Main Post Office on Kenyatta Avenue, Eleanor points to a group of women dressed in colourful robes. "Are those Swahili women?"

"No... those are Sudanese women. During WWII, Britain recruited many Sudanese soldiers to fight alongside the KAR (Kings African Rifles) in Burma. When the War ended, instead of repatriating them back to the Sudan, Britain offered them land to settle here in Kibera. The soldiers accepted the offer, and then brought out their wives and kids. In addition, there are a large number of Somali and Ethiopian refugees who fled strife in their countries and now live in Kenya permanently. Please add those to your list."

"I think I'll start my people-spotting at a more modest

level. Let me first try and find a thoroughbred *Mzungu*." Eleanor sounds self-confident. I am reassured that she is adjusting to the assortment of races, tribes, and colours that make up our population.

The next day is Sunday. Mum and Dad will host a lunch for the extended family to meet Eleanor at 1:00 P.M. However, Eleanor and I decide we can squeeze in an early morning excursion into the Nairobi National Park and still make it on time for lunch.

16

Wild Animals... Tame Family

I race our VW Beetle down a deserted Uhuru Highway and west along the Langata Road to the Main Gate. We arrive just as it opens at 6:30 A.M. There is already a line-up of six, four-wheel drive vehicles, three Kombi vans, and some private cars waiting to get in. We get out and view a large wall map of the park. It's a small park of only about forty-five square miles, shaped like a long arrowhead, with the sharp tip touching the Athi River. The north, east and south boundaries are enclosed by an electric fence. To the west of the park, the Mbagathi River carves its own natural boundary. On the other side of the river, running along its length, is the Kitengela Game Reserve.

"My Uncle Antonio, who you will meet today at lunch, used to bring Linda and me for occasional game-viewing into the park. Those were very special days and we looked forward to it. Mum used the promise of those trips as bribes to extort the completion of as many chores as she could from us. But it was always worth it."

"I remember reading in one of Karen Blixen's chapters; that European residents of Karen would ride out on horseback," Eleanor says. "This area was teeming with wildlife mixed with Masai cattle that grazed among them."

"This area was designated as a park only about twenty years ago, when the government moved the Masai and their cattle across the river to Kitengela. Do you realize that we're only five miles from the city centre?" I point out the Nairobi skyline. Since Independence, there are no more restrictions on the movement of people from rural areas. In fact, it has already started. Can you imagine what pressures there will be on this land in the years ahead? I wonder how the government will be able to resist that."

"As we drove here, I noticed the signs for the Langata Cemetery. I couldn't help thinking of the City of the Dead in Cairo. So many living, poor dwellers occupying that space? Probably more alive than dead now in that area," Eleanor laments.

"That's what urban planners are supposed to plan for.

"Okay, now my darling, concentrate and enjoy this little bit of paradise while it's still here. You will discover that spotting wildlife is more difficult than you imagine because they're so cleverly camouflaged to blend into the landscape."

I steer the Beetle up a side track, where only a few minutes earlier I had seen a UTC (United Touring Company) van turn. Just two hundred yards away, we encounter a group of vehicles that have encircled a pride of lions basking in the early morning sunshine. Eleanor is ecstatic.

We drive away from the group and, in the next ninety minutes, we see giraffes, zebras, a black rhino, buck and antelope, and at least twenty different species of birds. The noisy weaverbirds with bright yellow breasts and the superb starlings are an instant hit with Eleanor.

"We had better turn back now," I say looking at my watch.

We leave the Hyena Dam and head towards Songor Ridge. For much of the park, the terrain is gently sloping grass plain with a sprinkling of mainly acacia trees which supports plenty of grazing for the herbivores, which means fresh meat if you're a leopard.

"Lando... stop! Look over there." Eleanor is pointing to an acacia tree, also known as a 'yellow bark thorn tree'. In the deep shade of a strong overhead sun, a huge leopard is feasting alone on a freshly killed Thompson gazelle. I slowly edge the car closer to get a better photo. He looks up, warm red blood dripping from his whiskers. His sleek spotted skin shimmers through the grass. I click my photo. Eleanor gasps and closes her eyes. She cannot bear the sight of the blood on his jaw. She tells me that, although she had been to zoos and always knew the carnivores were fed on raw meat, she never imagined the brutality of it in the wild.

I drive north toward the main gate. We stop occasionally to photograph a crested crane, a pair of ostriches and some bushbucks. The recently completed David Sheldrick Sanctuary for orphaned elephants and rhinos is located next to the gate. The young animals, rescued when poachers kill the parents, are lovingly reared here before being relocated, where necessary. This is a reality, Eleanor loves.

After a quick clean up and change of clothes, we head to

Plums Lane, where a bevy of relatives are already assembled. Dad does the honours of introducing them to Eleanor in turn: "Your Uncle Antonio and Clara, Uncle Joe and Rose, Your first cousins Aurelio and Jill."

Dad hesitates as Jill, who is also from England, indicates that she has something to say. "Welcome to Kenya, Eleanor. I'm from Chester and I will tell you that it is a bit overwhelming at first. But even though I arrived here only last year, I feel as if Nairobi is truly my home."

Dad smiles warmly and continues. "It's a pity Uncle Rebelo and Margarida could not be here today. I know you have already met Uncle Renato, Anja's brother, and his wife Mavis in London."

"Yes, Eleanor has met both Uncle Renato and Aunty Mavis. They were at our wedding. They were your stand-ins. She has also heard of the assassination of Pio Gama Pinto," I say. I look at Eleanor to see if talk of murder and some people leaving Kenya is putting her off, but she seems to take the news in her stride. The introductions continue. Fortunately, Frank and the other children have been banished from the living room and are enjoying a picnic in the rear garden under the watchful eye of an ayah and Whiskey. The children are picnicking on the treasures from a huge peach tree and an enormous avocado tree.

It is after lunch in the late afternoon, when Eleanor gets to meet her first *Wananchi* on a one-to-one basis. As always, it is Whiskey that announces the guests. His noisy barking temporarily drowns out conversation indoors. I spot the 'intruder' approaching and ask Eleanor to please go onto the veranda to investigate. I follow discreetly behind.

A tall, lean African with distinctive features greets her with a smile and a gentle bow. He offers his right hand in a handshake, "Welcome, *Memsahib* Lando. I am Stephen Macharia. I wish to serve you and Bwana Lando forever. I have brought this gift for you from my mother." With that, he leans down and picks up a live chicken from a basket and thrusts it toward Eleanor. The chicken had not participated in a rehearsal. It squawks and flaps its wings, attempting to fly onto the roof, sending feathers into the air. Eleanor screams, turns a bright tomato red and steps back in shock, desperately looking around for me to rescue her.

"So, you have finally met the famous Stephen?" I say cheerily as I step forward to embrace Stephen.

"Yes, I have. Sorry, I just wasn't expecting to cuddle a live chicken in my best dress."

"It's the local custom to welcome someone special with a special gift. In fact, it's almost biblical; you remember the three wise men who took gifts to Bethlehem?" I chuckle.

"Sorry, luv, but I can't cope with anything live that flutters, squeaks, shrieks, or shoots out its tongue to catch insects and flies. I'm okay with spiders and furry caterpillars… and by the way, the wise men did not bring Baby Jesus smelly, squawky live chickens." She giggles.

Stephen, being left out of the conversation, interjects.

"Bwana Lando, how many cows did you pay to *Memsaab Erenol's* (Eleanor's) daddy? She is very beautiful." Eleanor blushes and exits to the kitchen to put together a platter of food for him.

I explain to Stephen that, unlike Kenyan customs, there was no payment for my bride. He's impressed with the great deal I've cut. Then he asks whether she can teach him to speak English if in exchange he teaches her Kikuyu. And he adds; "Memsahib is educated *Mzungu*, so she will earn much money for us."

Eleanor enters with a tray. She smiles as she watches her new friend gobble his lunch while speaking continuously on disjointed topics. Eventually Mum also walks in with a 'care package' for Stephen to take to his mother and sister. He finally departs with a reminder that, as soon as I have a job for him, he'll be ready to start immediately.

"What did he mean, 'earn money for us'? Do you have to support him? Is he thinking he will live with us?" Eleanor has grasped some bits of the conversation.

"Eleanor, I've known him since he was two-years-old and he feels he has nowhere else to go but to me. Anyway, let's talk about it later and see how we can find a solution. "But honestly my luv, this is not a good time."

We re-enter the living room to begin receiving warm farewells from the departing guests. I watch as she crosses the room to sit next to my mother.

A short while later, Eleanor is enjoying a quiet cup of tea and a chat with Mum. I'm explaining to Dad that I will resume work on Monday. Suddenly Frank, my six-year-old sibling comes bursting into the room. "Look Eleanor, these have fallen from our tree." He hands over two fine avocados, each weighing about two pounds. She's impressed and admits having seen them in grocery shops in England, but has never tasted one. Certainly, she had never seen them this size. Frank is beaming with pride for having introduced her to Kenyan avocados. She reaches out and thanks him with a hug which seals their friendship.

I'm relieved that Eleanor has now met most of the relatives and they all seem to love her.

Mum is particularly protective of her new daughter-in-law. She knows from her own experience how difficult it can be for a foreigner to arrive in a new country, faced with a new culture, and be expected to adjust and meld seamlessly into the community. I can overhear Mum recounting to Eleanor her own experience in 1935 when she first arrived in Kenya as a seventeen-year-old bride.

She spoke only Portuguese and the Goan dialect of Konkani. She had to learn English and Kiswahili as the two basic languages. The Indian *dukawallahs* (shopkeepers) used a lot of Hindi words, interspersed with English and Kiswahili. Her Sikh neighbour on Plums Lane, interspersed Punjabi words with Kiswahili, as she did not even attempt English at first. But Mum was proud of how she had overcome all the hurdles; to now speak English, have five grown relatively successful children, and a six-year-old who has just been awarded a prize for his 'elocution' in Standard One.

"We can go shopping on Tuesday in the Indian Bazaar. It's the best place for fabrics, spices and household goods," she says to Eleanor. "I will introduce you personally as my Lando's wife, so they won't take advantage of you. Since Independence, everything has become very expensive as the shopkeepers are trying to make as much money as possible, in case they are forced out of the country."

"Mum, you can't make general statements like that," I interject. I don't want Eleanor to buy into stereotypes. She should be able to enjoy and absorb what she gleans from her own experience.

"Lando, you have no idea what changes have taken place," Mum says. "You have been away."

As we are leaving, Frank sidles up to me and whispers, "Mum always tells me that eating avocados would make me big and strong. So, why is Eleanor so tall if she has never eaten avocados in England?"

17

Neighbours in Our Habitat

The honeymoon is over and now I'm torn between work and love. While single, I could work late into the evening to finish a project but now there's someone at home waiting for me. Our firm is busy, so I find myself watching the clock while racing to finish a current project and wanting to pack up for the day. With the post-Independence flow of investment money into Kenya, the construction industry is enjoying a boom after the years of stagnation during the Mau Mau period. Residential, commercial, industrial, private and public housing, office and factory space, all of it is in demand.

In the meantime, on the home-front, our personal paperwork is piling up and I'm having a panic attack.

I look at my personal 'to do' list and then to the clock and realize it's too late. The Immigration Office is now shut. I re-make my list for the next day:

1. Go to the Post Office to check up on a home telephone line. I've been on a waitlist for almost three weeks.

2. Go to the High Commission to pick up a British Citizen Registration form for Eleanor.

3. Go to the Immigration Office in Gill House on Moi

Avenue to process a request for her work permit.

It's 10:00 A.M. and I'm at the Immigration Office. The hall is crammed with anxious Asians preparing to emigrate to the UK and I'm anxious to get back to my desk. A man seated next to me tells me he's heard a rumour through a relative in Leicester that, "Britain is going to slam the gates shut for British Asians in 1968. Then we'll see how much more packed this office will be."

"Well, perhaps the Government should think about building a new immigration office," I cheekily reply. "One that's far more efficient."

"Did you know that this very building, Gill House, was taken over by the Government from a Sikh mill owner in Eldoret who did not pay his taxes? Imagine that?"

"I think that's good. Everyone should pay their taxes." There's a bit of annoyance in my reply which I'm hoping will put a stop to this man's endless monologue. But unfortunately, he continues.

"Now I hear, there's an important Kenyan politician who might be buying Gill House back from the Government." He also tells me that there are signs of corruption in some of the Government offices. I ignore him in the hope he's wrong about signs of corruption under President Jomo Kenyatta.

Finally, I get to pick up my blank forms and return to work.

I still need to go to another office to obtain a Driver's License application for Eleanor. She already drives, but an orientation to Kenyan road usage is obligatory. According to the local papers, the correlation between drinking and driving and the sharp increase in motor accidents is hardly surprising, as beer is sold by the case at petrol stations.

I am by nature an optimist, but back at the office, I have a little grumble about my tiring experience at Gill House. An English colleague and long-time Kenya resident empathizes with my anguish. He tells me there are many new laws introduced by the government since I left Kenya, but when I ask him for details, he says he's not sure exactly and frankly couldn't care less. He quietly adds that, to be on the safe side, he decided to move his family to Brisbane, Australia; although the Consulate has confirmed it will take another two weeks for his papers to arrive.

At breakfast the next day, I'm feeling a bit anxious, but doing my best not to show it. At the same time, Eleanor is preoccupied with her own burning issues.

"Where can I look for a record player, Lando? We made such a sacrifice to bring my records here; it seems silly not to be able to listen to them. I can't live without my music and my books. Oh dear, my books. Where shall I go to look for a bookshelf?"

"I'm glad you reminded me," I say cheerfully. "I'll deal with the record player, you look for the bookshelf, okay?" I don't have the heart to tell Eleanor we can't afford a record player. I don't want her to miss anything, or feel homesick for England. "I overheard you making plans with Mum about going out shopping today. Is that still on?"

"It's a bit iffy. She said she would get a message to me. And that reminds me… when are we likely to get a phone?" I understand that without a phone or driver's license, Eleanor is beginning to experience some symptoms of cabin fever.

"I'm working on it, darling." We exchange a kiss and a long hug. "Listen, if you're up to it, why not take a walk around the gardens and check out the neighbours. You never know who or what lurks behind the curtained windows."

"Don't worry about me, *Bwana*. I'll take a tour of the neighborhood, and tonight, I'll give you a full report on my day's adventures. I might even have a simple meal ready for you when you get home," Eleanor offers a smile and a cheeky salute.

It's about 6:00 P.M. I wend my way through traffic and finally return to our Delamere Flats complex. I catch a glimpse of Eleanor, sitting on a wrought iron bench under a Nandi Flame tree in full bloom. The low sun catches the higher branches, tingeing the leaves with a dash of orange against a lilac sky. The sun's rays reflect on the flowers and shrubs that surround my wife, causing them to glow as if they and she are encircled with halos. I stop mesmerized for a moment, soaking in the beautiful image I see before me. Her stillness and radiance makes me think of a magnificent sculpture set in a majestic European park. I breathe a gratifying sigh as I pull into our designated parking spot. She looks up, smiles and waves. There is no doubt, she is happy. She rushes toward me and delivers a warm, welcoming hug. "Come my darling, there are surprises in store for you tonight."

With that enticement, she quickly leads me inside and points with pride toward the dining table. It's beautifully laid out for dinner; draped in a navy blue, turquoise and black (*kitenge*) cotton cloth. Standing proudly at the centre is a glass vase that hugs several sunlight-yellow Gerber daises. The gleaming white plates and sparkling cutlery that bedeck the table are a gift from Mum and Dad. She giggles with delight at my speechless but joyful reaction.

"I think the table will prove to be grander than the very modest meal we're about to share," she cheekily suggests, "and that's mainly because I'm having a bit of trouble adjusting to the strange kitchen appliances I don't yet understand. But I do have one request, my darling… whenever it's possible, please can we switch to gas cylinders."

I want to jump in and promise her that she will have whatever she wants and needs by tomorrow; but I know it would be a false promise. Judging by my current income, we'll need to stay with the status quo until my financial options improve. So instead, I offer her the first platitude that come to my mind. "Everything in God's good time, my sweet. Everything in time."

She smiles and playfully tousles my hair. She already knows that change in Africa comes slowly.

She serves the first course.

Our lively dinner conversation seems to comfort and entertain both of us.

"Oh, Lando, I got a strange message from your Mum this afternoon through a neighbour, that I'm having some trouble decoding. Out of the blue, she says, 'since Independence, people generally recycle gifts because anything new and imported is too expensive.' Then she told me that we will be receiving gifts at our reception in three weeks. Now *Bwana*, if indeed there is some reception in the works, can you please tell me what reception she was talking about and how come I knew nothing about it?"

"Sorry, luv. It completely slipped my mind. I've been distracted since I pulled into the driveway tonight and was preoccupied when Dad phoned me at work earlier today. He called to remind me that since your folks insisted on having our wedding in England, Mum and Dad are going to host a reception for us here. They want you to meet their friends that are still here and haven't joined the Goan exodus as yet. I also gave him the names of some of my non-Goan friends from University and from work, and was assured it's not going to be a huge affair. Only about two hundred in all."

"Two hundred? That's a royal wedding in England! And I have nothing proper to wear. I even left my wedding dress behind to make room in our luggage for my books and records."

"Okay, Luv, how about we shop for a dress this Saturday? Or would you rather go with Mum?"

She tosses me a look that suggests it might be best that I accompany her on this royal wardrobe shopping adventure.

As the meal winds down over tea and biscuits, Eleanor has another surprise to share with me.

"About ten o'clock this morning, I heard a knock at the door. I opened it to find this very nice Sikh man, I'd say in his late fifties, who showed me a paper with your name and our address on it. He told me that the specially designed bed you ordered was downstairs in the lorry. I was so excited. Of course, I told him immediately to bring it up. I rushed to the bedroom and stripped down the two iron camp cots, folded the frames and set them aside."

"I sat and waited for what seemed like forever, until suddenly I heard a commotion outside. I looked out the living room window and saw the magnificent bed sitting on the street below. The Sikh was shouting orders to his two African helpers. A crowd had gathered and were gesturing, laughing, and seemingly offering advice. A European lady who, I discovered, lives upstairs from us started shouting from her window in a mixture of Kiswahili and English 'Please be quiet.' '*Hapana kelele.*' Joining the fracas in the street were two other ladies; one with a little boy in a stroller. Of course, by then my curiosity was bubbling over and I had to go down to see what the commotion was all about. Surely the crowd had seen a beautiful hand carved bed before."

"Oh my God, Eleanor, you're killing me with anticipation. Why didn't you tell me about the bed the minute I stepped out of the car?" I was as excited as a child about to meet Santa Claus for the first time. With that I ran to the bedroom to see for myself. The spot where our enchanted bed should be, was instead, a large, cold, empty space. I looked to my wife for clarity. She pointed to my left. My eyes followed and were now fixed on the two metal cots that were folded and propped against the wall.

"Darling, *hakuna matata* (no worries), they're just temporary," Eleanor offers to ease my pain.

"What... in hell... happened?" was all I could muster?

Eleanor patiently explained what the delivery man, Mr. Singh, had explained to her. 'The bed was fully assembled in our workshop. The joints were *bolted and glued solid. So, hard as we try, the bed cannot be maneuvered around the curved balustrade at the bottom of the stairs.*' So, after all the *kelele*, they put the entire bed back on the lorry and drove away. But Mr. Singh did say, '*I will come back, one day, tomorrow.*'"

"One day tomorrow? So we still don't know when we'll get to sleep in our fairytale bed."

"Yes, we do... One day tomorrow!" She giggled before adding, "But wait, there's one good thing that came from the crazy bed incident. After it was all over and the lorry had pulled away, I did get to meet and speak to several of our neighbours. So the whole experience wasn't a complete disaster. With all those diverse faces and languages out in the street, I think I'm beginning to learn to tell the difference between a Wageni and Mzungu."

"How's that?"

"Well, Diana is the mother of Jason, the two-year-old boy I mentioned who was in the stroller. She's a *Wageni*. Her husband John is a civil engineer with the PWD (Public Works Dept.) They're on a three-year expatriate contract, paid for by the British government. She says they were directed to a house, but instead chose an apartment for now, since it's cheaper and they have to save for a second car. She also intimated that she'd be afraid to be alone in the suburbs whenever her husband is away on business. They're both about our age, and guess what? She's from Stafford where I was born. Imagine that? They moved to Reading when she was six. She says we should have all the babies we want here, because *ayahs* are readily available and so affordable."

"Affordable maybe! But all in God's good time," I intervene. "I'm not ready yet for babies."

"I know, my luv. She was just being enthusiastic. She's so sweet. She said that after lunch, Jason sleeps while the ayah does the ironing; and during that time, she's free. So she kindly took me down to the Indian Bazaar. That's where I bought this *kitenge*. See, I didn't even call it a tablecloth. What do you think of our lovely *kitenge*?"

"Beautiful. They're all my favourite colours too."

"The older lady who was shouting out the window, was also very nice after all. Her name is Shirley and she's the *Mzungu*. She came downstairs and introduced herself during the *kelele*; and before she left, she insisted I come up to her flat to share a morning cuppa of chai. She lives alone, directly above us with her cat Safi which means 'clean' in Kiswahili."

"Yes, I met Shirley last week. Her face is a book of many untold stories, if someone has the time to listen. She seems lonely without her family here."

"Yes, that's her. She was born up-country, but was sent to boarding school in England at the age of twelve. Contrary to her parent's wishes, she returned to Kenya and married an old teen-age love. They had two boys and a girl. Her eldest son is now twenty. He followed a girlfriend back to her birthplace in

Northern Rhodesia. The second son migrated to Australia and the youngest girl is studying fashion and design in London."

"And the husband?"

"She candidly told me that she's not happy with him. She explained that anyone, who is not a citizen of Kenya, must now have a work permit. Her husband flatly refused to apply for one. The way she described him... I hate to say it, but he sounded like a racist. He tried to convince her to leave Kenya, but she couldn't bear the thought of leaving. So, one day, he disappeared and they never heard from him again."

"That's sad," I concur, "but I would suspect that it's due in great part to the stress of making major life-changes at their age. I heard about an ex-schoolmate from the Dr. Ribeiro Goan School who went to the UK during the exodus, just before Independence in 1963. Within six months, he had a breakdown and can't work anymore. What's worse is that his children are all very young, so it's really hard on the family."

"There are so many sad stories, Lando, but I have to admit, it was fun listening to Shirley speak. She uses a lot of Kiswahili words. English has become her second language," Eleanor concludes. "And you'll like this... she loves *Mzee* Jomo Kenyatta. Let me show you how she sounds. I had to write it down. '*When the watu (people) started all that Mau Mau matata (trouble) clamoring for Uhuru (Independence), so many of my kabila (kind) who call us Mzungu, just pulled up roots and started to leave. They could not imagine life under a Wanainchi (black) government. But I am a jua kali (hot sun) girl. A sunflower of the soil. Hapana - I will never leave Kenya.*'

"See how fast I'm picking up Kiswahili words? So, how did I do?"

"Splendid! I had no doubt you would pick it up fast. So again, which one is the *Wageni*?"

"Diana and *Mimi* are *Wageni*. You, my *tamu tamu*, (sweet) are a *Wahindi*. By the way, Shirley knows many Goans and had nice things to say about your people. She loves Goan food. She has been to Goan dances, but she didn't have a Kiswahili name for Goans and had never really thought about it. Her father employed an assistant farm manager and an accountant, both Goan. She had heard them referred to as the *karanis* (clerks), but always called them by their real, and easy to remember, Christian names."

"At this rate you will have completely mastered Kenya history and Kiswahili in a few weeks."

"Thank you for your vote of confidence. So anyway, that's how my day went my darling Lando. How was your day?"

"Ah, well, pretty normal, I'd say. There sure is no shortage of work… just a shortage of paycheck.

"By the way, Dad did mention that our reception at the Goan Gymkhana will be in three weeks. You'll meet most of the members that have not yet migrated to the UK, Canada, or to God-knows-where-else. Dad said they're all curious and excited to meet you. Also, Graham has invited us to lunch next Saturday at his new place in Gigiri. He wants to meet you and introduce us to his new partners and associates. Eleanor, my luv, our social calendar is filling up, and as you already learned, I might slip up, so would you mind keeping track of our engagements?"

While she mulls over my request and the calendar of events, I excuse myself to run down and pick up something from the car. Eleanor is about to see that she is not the only one with a surprise up a sleeve. I rush back in with her surprise tucked under my arm.

She's ecstatic over her new RCA record player and the new release of Frank Sinatra's recording of *Younger than Spring Time*. I don't bother to tell her that acquiring it was made possible by my good friend, Pius Menezes (Minicine Films Limited), who runs an electronics and film rental store on Government Road. I arranged to pay it off over time but he allowed me to take it *with no money down*. Pius had done the same for Linda and me in 1959, when we bought a black and white TV together for our parents. Of course there was a bit of collusion involved in our gift. We wanted to keep our Mum occupied, rather than have her sitting up worrying about Linda and me when we didn't arrive home on time, which I admit was not a rare occasion. As before, I extracted a promise from Pius that he would not breathe a word of the record player purchase to anyone.

We assemble the metal cots, bind them together and go to sleep to dream of fairy-tale beds, gas cylinders and electric blankets.

A couple of days later, I arrive home to the news that our new bed has definitely arrived, and is safely situated in its anticipated space. Everything went smoothly this time. No *kelele*. Eleanor is delighted with the design.

We happily and enthusiastically christened our fairy-tale bed that very night.

* *

The coming reception at the Goan Gymkhana has now become the focus of our attention. After shopping for dress fabric and balancing between a Goan tailor of ladies' clothes and my Mum's finishing touches, Eleanor is all set for the reception. The next three weeks are hectic with a flurry of details from catering to choosing an Emcee and toast speakers, and finding musicians. The big Goan bands of previous years are slowly breaking up, as more and more players leave to seek their fortunes in foreign lands, or to rejoin their families who have already left Kenya. Some families ended up in Canada others in the UK, Australia and Portugal.

* *

The reception day finally arrives. It is meant to be modest and 'in good taste.' Dad is a bit of a snob that way. My ex-buddies at the club who had, on numerous occasions in the past, been part of my volunteer team of 'decorators' for almost all social events, have taken responsibility for the décor of our event. About a dozen huge potted palms have been rented from the City's Parks Department. Some smaller flowering potted plants provide colour and Eleanor is delighted by the beauty of it all.

My parents have invited a diverse mix of guests. Most are friends from their generation along with their children of my generation. There are my ex-classmates from the Dr. Ribeiro Goan School who are members of a rival Goan Club. There's also an assorted mix of close Indian colleagues from my Technical High School days. And then there's my University and Work guests... and of course numerous relatives.

My dear clairvoyant friend and cellist, Braz Rodrigues, had rounded up three of his colleagues from the Kenya Conservatoire of Music to play the violin, clarinet and flute.

It's exciting to enter the hall to the spirited sound of light classical music. As the drinks flow during the evening, I can't help but notice the group's repertoire broadening and accelerating, between the speeches. They play a medley of international popular love tunes from Goa Portugal, East Africa, the USA and Europe that cover all flavours of music including the beautiful Swahili love song Malaika and they finish the evening with pulsating wedding polkas.

After Dad makes a speech welcoming Eleanor to our family and to the community, Mr. J. M. Nazareth, QC, a friend of the family, raises a toast to the couple. Graham McCullough joins in with a few words: "Eleanor, you have made two very good choices: The first was choosing Lando, and the second was choosing to spend your life in this beautiful paradise of Kenya."

There are many impromptu speeches throughout the evening. We travel the room together and manage to shake hands with every guest. Through it all, Eleanor seems a bit bewildered, not bothered, but maybe a little bewitched, as the Richard Rogers song goes.

And then, faster than it began... the evening is over.

On the drive home, I proudly share with Eleanor how delighted the friends and family were to meet her. "Now, that they know you, you'll have to face their persistent Goan hospitality. Everyone will ask you to make home visits and they will shower you with food, drink, gifts and advice."

"And that's supposed to be a bad thing, my luv?" She giggles. "Lando, I'm really appreciative, but I'm feeling uncomfortable, right now," she quietly admits.

"Why in the world would you be uncomfortable?"

"Do you remember you made that comment the other day, about my blue-rimmed glasses clashing with my turquoise dress? Well, I didn't want to embarrass you, so I left my glasses at home and smiled sweetly at every blur I was introduced to all evening. I don't think I'll recognize anyone I meet again. And they were all so gracious and welcoming. What shall we do?"

"We could have another reception in a couple of weeks. This time with your glasses on."

"Oh thanks a lot. I barely made it through this one without fainting from shyness."

* *

With the reception over, Eleanor and I must face a new reality in the weeks that follow. There are so many day-to-day personal issues for us to deal with, we become preoccupied with the details of survival while the changes in Kenya's transition to Independence go largely unnoticed.

The rent for our apartment consumes about eighty percent of my salary. While salaries in the private sector have gone up, they are still based on traditional racial differences. Civil servants are even more restricted in their salary ranges. In preparation for Independence, mountains of studies were carried out to try and figure out how to stabilize the cost of government administration. It was anticipated that an Independent government would be under immense pressure to create employment, and politicians would in turn, attempt to seduce voters by promising jobs that didn't exist. The worry was that they would then fashion a host of unneeded and unnecessary jobs in the public sector and discreetly offer them to their friends.

And now it seems that is exactly what is happening.

18

The Lows and Highs of Life... Begin

February, 1967

In the early morning, in preparation for my business trip with Graham, I parked my VW Beetle at the office, under the shade of a blazing flame tree, to await my return at the end of the day.

* *

It was a hot, tiring, dusty, and only partly productive trip. Graham and I were travelling in his car, now en route to Lanet on the outskirts of Nakuru, where Graham was to attend a brief meeting at the renamed Kenya Regiment Training Centre (5th Kenya Rifles) Headquarters before rushing through our final stops and turning toward home.

As we approached Lanet, we spotted a mass of people ahead, waving sticks and shouting at each other. It appeared as if the police were attempting to separate the mob into two groups. We could see that the ubiquitous nail-spiked road barriers had been dropped in place. It was a roadblock. Not so discreetly parked at the side of the road were two lorries loaded with men of the dreaded GSU (General Service Unit), dressed in full riot gear, awaiting orders to mobilize and crack a few skulls. It was their preferred method of *bringing calm* to a situation.

"I think we had better turn back," Graham says grimly. "I don't suppose you kept current with Kenyan politics while you were in the UK?"

"Not really. So, tell me, what's this all about?"

Graham's face is a sizzling burgundy. He slowly turns the car around, and then stomps on the accelerator. "We'll get out of here first, then I'll bring you up to date," he replies through gritted teeth. I have seldom seen him so angry.

Once out of view of the horde and the GSU, he speaks frankly of politics and his disappointment at the recent turn of events in the country. He still believes that President Jomo Kenyatta was, and is, the only man that could guide Kenya through those last steps to Independence. "With anyone else, we could have ended with a tribal and racial bloodbath that would tear the country apart." He explains how difficult it was for everyone when the economy plummeted during the period of the Mau Mau rebellion against the colonial government; and how, with the smooth transition, there has been a tremendous surge of foreign money for investment. He glances over at me. "Lando, I have been told that some of our clients are receiving confidential briefings from the British High Commission recommending they exercise caution in doing business deals.

"They've been warned that in the course of business discussions, they may be approached by individuals claiming to be emissaries representing one Minister or another. And that those 'representatives' have been instructed by Kenyatta to follow new directives. The clients are informed that there will be *additional fees required for facilitating* the set-up of new ventures. But plain and simple… I call it extortion!"

"But, are there any new laws to support those directives?" I nervously inquire.

"No. just 'informal' instructions. In other words, 'let it be known' that some people in high places are open to accepting bribes."

Graham looks at me to see if I'm shocked. But at that moment, my thoughts are with Eleanor at home alone. I had convinced her that Kenya was a peaceful paradise and would continue to be so under *Mzee* Jomo Kenyatta. It occurs to me that she's been rather nervous and looking a bit pale these past few days, so I'm beginning to think that she's already heard something from the neighbours and is not telling me. I sigh as I focus on our mutual need to protect each other.

"I'm actually relieved, Graham. I thought you were going to inform me that we're on the verge of a civil war. I'd read in the English papers that *Mzee* had sacked his Vice-President, Oginga Odinga last year and had replaced him with Joseph Murumbi. I wasn't sure what the outcome would be from that move."

"Murumbi is a wonderful, educated man with much worldly experience… but sadly he resigned after only nine months. Our current Vice President, Daniel Arap Moi, was appointed on the 5th of January, 1967 less than two months ago. I fear that what we're being fed is starting to taste like a smelly stew of matata with incipient corruption."

"Here we are," Graham says as he pulls up at the gatehouse. We have arrived at our next destination. Here we will complete a survey of the age and condition of buildings and infrastructure at the erstwhile British Army Barracks in Gilgil, which is about twenty miles from Nakuru.

"No political gossip now," Graham warns as we enter the building.

While completing our task, an official engages us and informs us that, "most of the British troops have moved out, but there's a rumour that Kenya has signed a long-term contract for British troops to undertake joint training exercises in Kenya."

Neither of us offers a response; but I'm thinking, that Britain's offer is not for altruistic motives, but is probably more to ensure security of their lives and their economic interests in Kenya.

We say our respectful goodbyes and head to the car. Politics is not even mentioned on our drive back to Nairobi.

* *

My Beetle is where I left it, except now it's covered in petals and bird droppings.

Dusk is that brief moment of light before night comes down like a curtain, engulfing all in the blackness of an African night. I drag my tired body onto the sweltering driver's seat and wind down the windows.

The air is filled with the excited tweeting and chirping

of birds exchanging news of their day. Soon the crickets will take over and sing through to daybreak. Guard dogs argue in the distance … their barks reverberating through thick waves of heat. It's the same every night in that window of twilight, so near to the Equator. I tilt my seat back and close my eyes and imagine what news I could tweet of my world today, if I were a bird.

I turn the key in the ignition, close the windows, lock the doors, and head back to the Delamere Flats and Eleanor. I watch headlights converge, like moths to a flame. The neon encrusted Nairobi Casino on Museum Hill is lit up like Las Vegas. The birth of a new Kenyan nation in 1963 has brought lavish showers of foreign cash into the country. It seems that the Western Alliance countries like Britain, USA, Germany and France have been competing with the Eastern Bloc of Russia and its satellites, to ingratiate themselves with infusions of cash to the new Administration.

As I approach our door, I can hear Vivaldi's *Four Seasons* playing in the background. On entry, an aromatic joss stick is emitting a wisp of smoke, reminiscent of our student days.

Eleanor is waiting for me, still looking a bit pale and nervous. "Sorry, I'm late, luv." I hug her and plant a quick kiss. "I missed you so much. How was your day?"

"Mixed," she says. "Your friend Amy came around unannounced and insisted on treating me to lunch at the Panafric Hotel. She's a right old chatter-box. She said your regular drinking chums at the Goan Gymkhana miss you. She wants me to bring you back to the Club. She says it would help me feel more comfortable and welcome among Goans. That woman doesn't miss a beat. Can you believe she even noticed that I was squinting at the reception and assumed I was trying out a new set of contact lenses?"

"Did you come clean?" I tease.

"Yes. She laughed when I told her the truth. She seems engrossed in the minutiae of every Goan's life. She knows little details about everybody; like, who drinks too much, who's leaving, who's staying… "

"… But the fact is, my luv, she's really kind and good-natured and can hold her liquor better than most men. I hope you made it clear that we, in particular, don't drink much because we can't afford to drink on my salary." Eleanor smiles and takes my hand.

"I'm sorry, sweetheart, but we're going to afford it even less now because Lando darling, I'm pregnant… I… you… we… we're expecting a baby."

"Baby? A baby? You're… you're… pregnant?" I stammer and stutter and hug her. I'm happy and shocked. "That's wonderful my darling. How did it happen?"

"Really my luv, you don't know how it happens?" She giggles that enchanting giggle and I melt and hug her again and again and again.

At least I now understand why she's been looking so pale and seeming so nervous these past few days. "Have you told Mum?"

"Well that's an interesting question. I was over at Plums Lane last week to learn a recipe for preparing *Xacuti* (a special

Goan dish) from her. As I was chopping onions, I suddenly had to rush to the bathroom. I was throwing up like an erupting volcano. It turns out your mum knows about these things. So she told me that I must go and see Doctor Masie and I did. And since Dr. Masie is a gynecologist, the answer to your question is that your mum actually knew before I did."

"Wow, that's incredible." I pull up a dining chair and sit down as close to her as the chair would allow.

"Oh, I have more good news for you, Lando! Stephen came round today and he's actually making a serious effort to speak English. He's dropped the 'Memsaab' and insists on calling me 'Miss' Erenol. But what he really came for was to see if you've found a job that can support him, and I suppose his mother and sister! I'm worried. I mean, what we are going to do about him?"

"I'm worried too, luv … but he has no one else he can turn to."

"Lando, darling, I must be honest, I'm beginning to get a little anxious about living in Kenya. Amy warned me we should be careful going out after dark because security is becoming a problem. And Amy tells me, many Goan families are planning to go to the UK and Portugal, or back to Goa. Other Asians are leaving too. She says it's about the new government policy. From now on all jobs will go to black Africans, not brown or white Kenyans."

"There are rumours, yes. There's a lot of wild gossip being spread around, but I believe that everything will be okay and as you meet more people, you'll be able to judge for yourself.

Maybe you should mix more with the *Wageni* crowd. They're more our age and are here for the African experience. They live for the moment and enjoy themselves. They're less worried about changing times and are not forever nostalgic about the good old days."

I decide not to tell Eleanor about Graham's comments on the emerging matata in Kenyan politics.

Over dinner, we talk and talk about buying some needed household items, seeing more of the Nairobi countryside, perhaps buying a second car, maybe planning a trip to the coast... but mostly we talk about how our lives will change with a baby on its way.

"Lando, I'd really like to find some professional work, otherwise I'll be wasting my education. And we could use the extra income." Eleanor suggests.

"You have the job offer from the University. We just need the work permit to come through. As my mum would say; we 'have to learn the art of being patient'." I offer an easy smile and she leans her head on my chest.

"Come my luv, let's go to bed."

* *

"Lando, are you awake, darling?"

"I am. Oh my God, what's wrong?"

"Nothing. I was just thinking that my mum might want to come out to visit."

"Eleanor, it's four in the morning. It's too early for this conversation. Listen to me, my luv, our baby won't be here for another eight months or so, therefore, no need for your mum to rush here. Besides, before any of that happens, we'll need larger accommodation. Now, my little worry wart, please go back to sleep."

* *

A week later I'm summoned to meet with an Immigration Officer over Eleanor's work permit. He explains politely, if somewhat laboriously, that the Government had passed legislation requiring all non-citizens to apply for work permits. The purpose is intended to ensure more Kenyans are employed in jobs previously carried out by non-citizen Asian and European residents. He quotes excerpts: "As a rule, permits are only given to spouses of the principle permit holder, who have special skills that are unavailable in the country. A policy for the spouses of Kenyan nationals has not yet been specified." He suggests we meet again, in the hope that he "may have some good news."

We have no option but to continue to be patient.

19

Anxiety Becomes the Norm

Eleanor's increasing angst over Nairobi's deteriorating security seems to have ebbed. The anticipation and excitement of our first baby is palpable, however, the "weather" map of her pregnancy is dotted with cyclones of uncontrolled energy, low pressure fatigue, followed by gusts of unpredictable mood swings.

Mum takes me aside to counsel me on my anxiety over Eleanor's issues. "You must have patience, Lando. These are all common but temporary problems during pregnancy. It will all be over in a few weeks," she calmly assures me. "The moods... the morning sickness... Eleanor's sudden rejection of mangoes and other fine foods... and the cravings. They will all go away in time. Be patient! "

"Mum, I've been doing my best to keep up with her ever-evolving cravings. I brought her Scottish Shortbread and Bassett's Liquorice Allsorts from Bishendas Brothers at the Municipal market. And I even found her favourite newspaper the *Manchester Guardian Weekly* at the newsagent in Westlands."

"Good," my mum replies, "you must keep doing your best,

and in a few months you'll see it will have paid off nicely when you welcome a healthy baby into your world and a happy wife back into your life." She concludes with a twinkle in her eye and a reassuring hug. "Remember... patience, Lando."

* *

My encounters with clients, and an overlapping contact with expatriate experts, gives me a new perspective on the changes that are taking place in the country.

The daily news headlines carry multiple reports of political fund-raising events, inauguration of new businesses, and ribbon-cutting ceremonies by the Mzee and his Ministers. They give the impression of a strong confident Kenya Government now in control. The disruption of Asian economic activity; the prolonged turmoil within the white farming community; the uprooting of white and brown families and the tragic upheaval of personal dreams and aspirations is the white noise of a colonial system being expunged.

There is a new sound and a new rhythm that is muffling the white noise. It is the happy, excited fusion of a relatively young, motivated, educated, colour-blind society in the making. The *Wageni* are a multi-cultural, multi-national, multi-colored mix of temporary residents. They are also referred to as *Expatriates*. They are visible everywhere. They come from abroad to work and to see Africa. They are inspired by the exuberance and exhortation of the youthful US President Kennedy. Energized by the enhanced budgets of the Peace Corps, CUSCO etc., some have come as volunteers with youth development programs, others are employees of international and bi-lateral aid agencies; each with their cryptic acronyms. Local technical consulting firms expand and bring in more consultants and professional experts. And many are employees of multinational corporations. But the one thing they all have in common is that they want to make a difference in people's lives. These young ambitious minds had hitherto only known Africa by what they saw and heard on television and radio.

Kenya's strategic geography bordering on Somalia, Ethiopia, South Sudan, Uganda, and the Congo Republic has the potential for being the best listening post for rival cold-war spies. We notice a sudden influx of 'diplomats' and their families.

I envisage the constant movement of visiting *Wageni*, as analogous to the spectacle of the annual wildebeest migration across the Masai Mara and Serengeti, which in turn attract predators that accompany the herds and feed off of them. As for their human predators or con-men counterparts, they too attract prostitutes, pimps, old style preachers and new style evangelists. They migrate into Nairobi, Mombasa and Kisumu and the smaller townships. They have all flocked to celebrate, contribute and partake of Kenya's newfound wealth and freedom.

The *Wageni* have brought their families along, which means they have the wherewithal to voraciously consume local and imported goods and services. Almost overnight, the cultural transformation of big cities like Nairobi is complete. Shops are stocking foods and specialty items from a range of different countries. New restaurants that cater to different palates are opening in abundance. Bars and Nightclubs proliferate. It is now a vibrant, bustling, multicultural city.

Eleanor and I have many Goan friends who intend to stay. A number of senior Goan civil servants have been requested to remain to help with the transition... to train Kenyans to take over their jobs. Goan teachers are in high demand. Goan secretaries, who have always been in demand, feel they might stay on until they see how members of their extended families make out in the UK, Canada and Australia. Others have sensed new opportunities opening up and are ready to start new businesses in Kenya.

Eleanor and I are most impressed with Betsy Pinto and her husband, Richie.

"We knew we had to do something," Betsy explains. "I had a good job with Barclays Bank and I did some part-time work with Francis Drummond Limited, Stockbrokers."

"I was with Shell," said Richie. "Nothing there for me now."

"So we went on a quick trip to check out life in England. Our friends had a good life in Kenya but they left before Uhuru. We saw how our close friends were struggling over there," Betsy continues. "They worked long hours, had to prepare school snacks for their children, wash dishes by hand, they did laundry twice a week, attended night classes, and washed their car on weekends. Sunday Mass was the only social life they had but many were so tired by the weekend, they skipped more masses than they attended."

"So we came back and opened *Beezee Secretarial Bureau*," Betsy declares triumphantly. "We haven't looked back since."

"Weren't you worried about bringing up your children here?" Eleanor uneasily asks.

"Like all parents, we do everything possible to give them a better life," Betsy says. "We realized we could still send them to boarding schools in the UK for a first class education, and that was enough to calm our fears."

These conversations seemed to help allay some of Eleanor's apprehension. Mum, who sensed my anxiety, told me with a first pregnancy there's a lot to be worried about.

Eleanor has made friends among the *Wageni*. Each day brings new discoveries. She had no previous experience of a colonial lifestyle in the tropics, having been born and raised in England; so every night a new tale is recounted with relish at our dinner table.

"Lando, do you know that almost all the *Wageni* live in roomy three bed-room bungalows on large plots of land with beautiful gardens? Shirley took me to see a friend in Karen who lives on five acres, has four dogs, and employs a fleet of servants?"

I point out that Kenya's residential apartheid created this land-use pattern of distribution and it's not the fault of the *Wageni*. "This is the only housing available to them outside the 'African locations' and 'Asian areas.' That's how non-European residential estates are labelled."

"I didn't imagine each family would employ so many just for cleaning and washing," she says.

"Employing people is a social responsibility in Africa. When we can afford it, we too, will employ someone," I reply. "There are not enough jobs available for everyone."

**

Patience wins the prize. Finally, there is news on immigration and work permits. The new legislation has been signed by President Jomo Kenyatta. It requires the Government to toughen the rules and improve enforcement. It includes a provision for foreign spouses married to Kenyan nationals to obtain work permits, if the jobs they do cannot be filled by qualified Kenyans and if their expertise will help to improve Kenya.

In late March, Eleanor finally receives a work permit along with an offer of employment at the newly-established Housing Research Unit at the University which is managed by a Danish team under a bi-lateral aid project. The idea of an extra salary, is as pleasant a sound to the ear as Sinatra singing *"But Not for Me."* Eleanor will be paid at the local salary rate… but the good news is… she begins immediately.

Now we're faced with another problem. We have only one car and we don't always have the exact same work hours. A couple of times a week, Eleanor manages to get a ride into town with our neighbour… but the fact is, we're going to need a second car.

**

Over the next few weeks, we juggle our time between her work and mine, house hunting and taking short trips to national parks and other scenic spots. As we travel around the country, Eleanor is amazed by the sheer natural beauty and bounty of the land that Kenya offers and the unevenness with which this bounty is distributed. This in-flowing wealth is bound to reduce the plight of the poor. At least that's what we both hope.

Even with the support of Eleanor's added income, I have this growing anxiety eating at me. A problem is gnawing at my insides and I'm beginning to recognize the sensation.

Years ago, when I was attending boarding school in Goa, I developed a persistent edginess and I felt an overwhelming urge to be set free. It was how I imagine a caged animal must feel when it paces the constricting fence that limits its freedom. It paws away at potential gaps in the enclosure to no avail. This mood did not go away until I engineered my escape from Goa and return to Kenya.

This time I could not quite pinpoint the solution… but the problem was palpable.

* *

Graham asked me to join him on a site visit to the Mount Kenya Safari Club in Nanyuki. When we were finished, he suggested an early lunch before heading back to Nairobi.

"Lando, we're going to be advertising for building contractors to submit bids for the construction of the Mahe Beach Hotel in the Seychelles." He must have seen the look of panic on my face.

"No, I wasn't going to ask you to go," he says, with a grin. "Not with Eleanor expecting a baby. But my Saudi client has asked me to open a local office there and personally supervise the project. So Pat and I gave it some serious thought, and I've accepted the position."

"I don't quite understand. Does this mean you'll open a branch in the Seychelles? Or do you plan to close down the firm here?" I ask nervously. The thought that now flashes like streak lightening through my mind is of me being unemployed.

"The Seychelles will be a separate entity," he says. "It will be too complicated with all the changes under way to restructure our firm."

Perhaps he sensed my surprise and distress at the news.

"I wanted to tell you this personally, Lando. The Partners have met and discussed you taking on a major responsibility in shaping our future practice. In this connection, we will be adjusting your salary substantially upwards as soon as you begin. I imagine it will be useful with the new baby arriving. Of course you'll want to share the news with your wife," he declares. He seems self-assured and content with the offer.

I thank him for letting me know and for thinking of me for the position.

* *

After lunch, we head for the Nanyuki airstrip. The pilot carries out the routine pre-flight checks on the small Cessna and we take-off heading for Nairobi. The plane makes a wide arc approaching Nairobi from a different direction to the east, keeping well away from the JKIA (Jomo Kenyatta International Airport) flight corridors to the south. We glide over Thika, Ruiru, and the housing areas to the east and south.

I see that the whole area is transforming into a sea of corrugated iron roofs. Close up, Mathare Valley is like a giant patchwork quilt of corroded rusty browns and shiny grey aluminum squares where new construction has sprung up to fill in the last of the open spaces.

In that moment, I am struck with the overwhelming thought that I must do something to change the African housing model they've been using since colonial times. It was always my ambition to improve housing conditions for the poor. I realize that Graham's firm can't possibly attract a public client who will be responsible for providing housing for the poor. Only public agencies will do that. I could leave the firm and join City Hall, but they can't provide me with a living wage.

Now I'm stuck on the uncomfortable horns of a dilemma. If I choose to stay with Graham's company, I'll never get to improve housing conditions for the poor; but if I go to work for the government, I might possibly fulfill that ambition… but will not be able to support my family.

We land safely and I drive home having added gallons of anxiety to my already full tank.

* *

On the domestic front, we have a new reality. Our third-floor-walk-up days must come to an end as Eleanor's pregnancy advances. We will need more room for the baby; more space for doing laundry, and accommodation for an ayah.

On our weekends away from work, we set out on a desperate house-hunt only to find the search becomes more and more distressing. The *Wageni* have raised the cost of rent because of increased demand, especially for the northern and western areas of Nairobi. Everywhere that is acceptable to us is not affordable for us. Houses of émigré Europeans and Asians are being bought by the new African middle-class who are either politicians or occupy top civil service jobs. The homes are then selectively offered to higher-paying *Wageni*, who are willing and able to pay up to five years' rent… in advance.

Eventually, we heard from a *Wageni* couple that a place has just gone up for sale on Peponi Road (Marlborough Road). Kitisuru Road runs along the ridge facing the property.

We made an appointment to view the house, which is on a lovely isolated location at the end of Peponi Road. It's a small, stone, fourteen hundred square foot bungalow, on three and a half acres of land, overlooking a ravine. It also has a detached two-room servant's quarters. The owner is anxious to sell and has priced it reasonably, as compared to all the other places we've seen. I'm already imagining how, one day, I can completely transform the house; expand it and build a cantilevered deck over the ravine. I remember the American Architect, Frank Lloyd Wright and his design of Falling Waters. I quietly mention my idea to Eleanor.

"Whoa there mister, you haven't bought it yet," she whispers.

I turn to the agent and without ceremony, I declare: "We'll take it for the asking price."

We put down a deposit and have a month to raise the rest

of money that's required. We have no credit history and our joint salaries are still low. However, to our delight, after supplying names of three guarantors, we're able to secure a loan from a housing Finance company.

A week after the sale is formalized, we discover, from our soon-to-be neighbours, that the property we just purchased had been the favourite target of armed *panga* (machete) gangs that had broken in and robbed the place three times in the previous eight months. Now, the isolation factor doesn't seem quite so attractive.

* *

Stephen has been maintaining contact with Mum and Dad to keep up with news of my career progress, which he seems certain will resolve *his* job search. He is present with Mum and Dad when we break the news about our move.

Stephen listens carefully. His eyes sparkle. He looks at Eleanor then turns to me and tells me that God has sent us this opportunity so we can be together again because now he has an employment offer for us. His offer is to move into the servants' quarters, take full responsibility for maintenance of the acreage and start a vegetable garden.

Within two months, Eleanor, Stephen and I have made the move into our new house. By that time, a 'bush telegraph' among our acquaintances has been ignited. Six highly-referenced and experienced *ayahs*, each willing and available to relocate nearer the baby's due date, have left their phone numbers.

In advance of welcoming our first born, we are faced with

an adoption. Cloto, a Rhodesian ridgeback was reared at the Kenya Regiment camp at Gilgil and was handed down through at least three owners in as many years. Our Wageni friends do a masterful job of selling the "adoption" idea to my pregnant and vulnerable wife with this pitch: "British troops in Kenya are going to be substantially reduced and we have to find a good home outside the camp for this hero dog, or… he'll be put to sleep."

Eleanor, who immediately fears for the dog's life while assuming personal guilt over the reduction of British troops, insists we adopt Cloto.

In the space of two months, we have now acquired some of the attributes of a stable middle-class Kenyan family: mortgage, acreage and a big *mbwa kali* (savage dog.) To add to all that, we have Stephen, and soon an ayah on our payroll, but what we don't have is the income of the *Wageni*.

20

Patience Is Indeed a Virtue

Stephen is waiting, one evening, by the entrance to our property on Peponi Road as I arrive home. He begs me follow him into the garden.

Ours is a steeply sloping lot, with a coarse stone-paved driveway lined with Nandi Flame trees and edged with a row of agapanthus (African lily), and yellow and orange coloured daylilies. It's a glorious blaze of colour; shades of red in the trees, blues tinting to purple, highlighted by yellow and orange daylilies that bloom together from January to March.

It's a driveway worthy of a four-thousand square-foot mansion, rather than our fourteen-hundred square-foot cottage built in hand-hewn Nairobi grey stone topped with a Mangalore tile roof. The cream-painted metal-framed casement windows covered with heavy wire mesh burglar-proofing do nothing to enhance its appearance. The area immediately around the house is level, with parking space for four cars at the end of the drive.

At one time, bountiful coffee bushes had been hacked down to clear the land of the once working coffee plantation, leaving only a few spiked stems with their roots intact.

The main contributing factor in our decision to choose this house was the sight of two majestic and ethereal, lacy, lilac-blue Jacarandas that gracefully stand watch at our front entrance.

Our front door opens directly onto a tiny patch of grass that's about fifteen-feet by twelve. Eleanor thinks this patch of grass will be lovely for the baby, if we can find some way of keeping her or him from falling over the edge and down to the stream below. I reassure myself that my plan for building terraces will mitigate that risk.

Rich, red soil covers the land, which means that keeping Cloto's dirty paw-prints out of the house has become Eleanor's obsession.

Stephen has a dream and a plan. He tells me that by the time he's finished with the fruit and vegetable garden, he (and I) will be supplying the local markets with tons of fresh produce, weekly. He informs me that he will need some money and a *fundi* (tradesman) to help install irrigation pipes along my proposed terraces. He thinks a small chicken run between his quarters and the main house can supply us with all the eggs we'll want, and "once in a while maybe a chicken for Miss Erenol to cook."

I'm very impressed with Stephen's initiative. I do not wish to discourage him, so we talk about doing the development in stages. "Stephen, why don't you start with a small patch of garden, and when that's done we'll find a *fundi* to help you build a chicken house." He seems content with the compromise. I'm proud of his determination and creativity but I'm still filled with sadness over the despicable racist actions that sent that seven-year-old boy to a detention camp; and deprived this inherently intelligent young man of even a primary school education.

He confides in me that he has tried to discuss some important things in relation to the garden with Miss Erenol, but she is preoccupied with planning for our baby.

He insists: "Bwana, you must to warn Miss Erenol about the Kikuyu man who will come to her door to offer to dig up *dudus* (termite queens) from your ground. That man is *mkora* (crook). He bring the 'queens' in Bata shoe box and say he dug them from earth and she must to pay him to rid them. Miss Erenol must not to pay him. She must let me to beat him."

* *

Patience wins out.

Eleanor recovers from her early pregnancy symptoms. She is up and about, wishing to do and see as much as she can before the baby arrives. It's not an easy prospect without a second car.

* *

On May 22, 1967, the Goan Gymkhana celebrates its 31st Anniversary. This by tradition, is one of our two annual black-tie dinner dances. The other is the New Year's Eve Dance. Both are usually popular and crowded events, however, unlike previous years, there is not a heavy demand for tickets. A slow, out-migration has quietly been taking place since Independence, as young Goans are opting to seek a future elsewhere. Some older Goans with young children also seem to be leaving. I'm concerned that Eleanor, seeing the exodus, may become anxious again.

I need not have worried.

As we chat over a hot chocolate nightcap, Eleanor cheerfully shares a revelation with me. "I bumped into Betsy Pinto and Richard today and they said that their business is really booming now. And they also told me that many other Goans are staying and feeling optimistic for the future."

"That's good news, luv," I say. "I met today with Orlando and Zenin, my ex-schoolmates and they've started a printing company on Tom Mboya Street (Victoria Street). They also feel that everything should be okay here, especially as there was no *matata* in Kenya at Independence."

* *

An opportunity for a road trip down to Mombasa appears out of the blue. Graham has asked me to check the progress on an ongoing project in Mombasa… and best of all, I can take Eleanor along with me. She's ecstatic at the prospect of going down to the coast and dipping her toes in the Indian Ocean. "This is a perfect time, my luv, because in a few months I'll be too big to squeeze in and out of the Beetle," she says with a giggle.

We plan an easy trip that will include many stops on the way and will avoid as much of the main road between Nairobi and Mombasa as possible. Lorry and car traffic has increased substantially since I last drove that route in 1963 and little has been done to straighten the road alignment, or repair bad stretches. Newspapers report there are government plans to do just that, but no indication, when this will happen.

We make an early start.

We're just past the airport going south on the Mombasa Road, when Eleanor pulls out a handkerchief and presses it to her mouth and nose. I feel a slight panic rising until she assures me that it's not her nausea returning, it's the stench emanating from the Kenya Meat Plant at Athi River. I smell it, but as I've passed this way for so many years, my olfactory seems immune to the perfume.

We leave the nasty odour far behind as we race over the Athi Plains. The sight of the green grass shimmering after recent rains is one of the unforgettable magnificent images of Africa. It's a miracle of nature, that dry, parched, grassy plains can simply turn vivid green overnight.

"Lando, look at the zebra and deer over there," Eleanor shouts.

"Many years ago, Dad talked about the massive herds of animals everywhere, grazing lazily, as the trains went past. He was amazed that they always appeared unperturbed by the roar of the steam engines. There are far less of them now but they still seem unperturbed."

Soon we arrive at the Tsavo Gate by the river, heading towards Mzima Springs. We are barely half a mile from the gate inside the Park when Eleanor whispers loudly, "Lando, look! Elephants! Red elephants!"

The red dust of Tsavo covers everything in its path, including the elephants. She points to the Chuyulu Hills on the horizon and ponders; "I always thought of elephants being the dark-grey colour of those hills."

I add to her colour quandary, when I promise her a trip to Amboseli National Park on the Tanzania border, where the elephants are a uniform pale grey blue as a result of the geological volcanic upheaval that created the Rift Valley thousands of years ago.

Eleanor abruptly grabs my arm and insists I stop the car!

A giant porcupine, its sharp bristles erect as if a lion or cheetah had just attacked it, darts onto the red compacted murram track. It is a laterite soil with a high level of iron oxides. We watch the porcupine lumber safely across the path before we continue on our way.

Meanwhile, the sun is beating down on a landscape of sparse thorn trees and low scrubland, punctuated by giant baobabs that are trees that look like they've been uprooted and replanted upside down. The stark beauty of the landscape overwhelms Eleanor. "I had not imagined anything like this," she says. Her face is glowing a brilliant pink from the heat. I turn at the wooden signpost that reads 'Mzima Springs.' Within minutes, we are in a glade of yellow-bark thorn trees, palms, papyrus, elephant grass, and other greenery. An oasis in the middle of nowhere. It's teeming with birdlife. This is the miracle of the Chyulu Hills. The water flows underground in a gushing river that bubbles up in springs forming a deep pool. The Park Authority built an underwater viewing window, through which visitors can see an abundance of swimming fish, turtles and sometimes even hippos. A short walking distance, along well-defined paths (as protection from the wild animals that use the springs as a watering place,) is another glade of trees. Elegant storks and graceful blue herons stroll leisurely by while in the same vicinity, we spot, two foreboding looking crocodiles, several obese hippos and a ballet of gazelles.

We are in no hurry. We choose a safe and comfortable spot and settle down for a picnic. I want Eleanor to fully absorb the magic of this beautiful country where, within a few hours ride from Nairobi, the ever-present problems of security, immigration permits, or making ends meet, simply melt away.

Eventually we make our way toward our car, stopping on the way to study a map that shows how water from Mzima Springs is channeled into a large pipeline that relies on gravity to supply the coastal town and Port of Mombasa with its fresh water needs and still has more to spare.

Following a brief restroom visit and a snack at the Inn at Mtito Andei, we continue on to Mombasa to arrive before sunset. Each rail station along the way, was built over fifty years ago to provide water-filling depots for thirsty steam engines. They bear familiar names and are key distance markers to road-based traffic: Sultan Hamud, Emali, Makindu, Kibwezi, Mtito Andei, Tsavo, Manyani, Voi, Mackinnon Road, Mariakani and Mazeras.

The simmering heat radiates in waves from the corrugated metal barracks of the Manyani Detention Camp we pass en route. As we drive slowly by, I can't help but think of Stephen and his family and the nightmare they suffered through.

I look over at my radiant wife who seems to be in a trance. In spite of the fan blasting cool air from the dashboard, it appears that the heat is getting to her. I stop the car. "Eleanor, are you awake?"

"I am. I was just enjoying the meditative ride."

I breathe a sigh of relief.

"Sorry to interrupt, but do you see that large encampment over there? It was built by the British to detain 'hard-core' prisoners during the Mau Mau uprising. When Stephen's father and family went missing in 1954, Dad went around to all his Goan Police contacts seeking some clues to their whereabouts."

"So, is that where Stephen's father was sent?" she solemnly asks.

"Mr. Azavedo, Dad's close friend at the Criminal Investigation Department was not really certain. In fact, the Government kept very tight control over which officers worked on the detention files. Dad believes only the *Wazungu* officers were given quick security clearance. Mau Mau detainees were first put through an initial interrogation in Nairobi, at the Langata Barracks. The women and children were sent to different settlement villages around the country. Men, judged to require further interrogation, were sent here at Manyani and to Mackinnon Road a few miles ahead. Out here they could not be physically reached or contacted by their friends or supporters from the Kikuyu areas. Soon these camps became overcrowded. No one knows if any records were kept, if anyone received any legal help, or if severe sum-mary justice was indiscriminately meted out. In later years, there were rumours of the despicable conditions in the camp and how the prisoners were forced to dig graves for fellow inmates who died of abuse or starvation inside those walls."

"That's horrid! So you believe this is where Stephen's dad died? Did the incoming Kenyan Government do anything about these atrocities?"

"I've been away and out of touch, I don't know. But from time to time, a news item will appear about what a raw deal the 'freedom fighters,' as those then 'terrorists' are now called, have received from the Kenyatta Administration.

"Ah, but let's talk of other things, my darling. We're supposed to be on a matata-free journey."

She smiles in agreement. I start the car and move on.

"See those hills ahead? They're the Taita Hills, and the glorious plain below is a wonderful section of Tsavo West Park... but we'll have to leave that for another trip. It's not on our schedule."

We drive over the Makupa Causeway that links the mainland to the Island of Mombasa. A short while later, we're crossing the Nyali Bridge heading north. It's about 5:00 P.M. when we pull into the magnificent portico of the Nyali Beach Hotel.

It's pure luxury to wash off the day's dust, change into clean soft cotton evening wear, and sip a long cold drink on the terrace of the hotel. The terrace, set high up on a promontory of coral, offers beautiful views of Old Town Mombasa and large colonial mansions.

The pink sky turns slowly to a bright orange as the sun disappears over the island.

An overnight stay at this beautiful hotel and its stunning view of Mombasa was the big surprise that I had managed to keep secret from Eleanor.

* *

That night, we eat a magnificent dinner cooked by staff once trained by a top Goan Chef who retired to his beloved island of Goa. It was sheer coincidence that night that the famed Goan pianist Edmund Silveira and his four-piece combo were making a guest appearance at the hotel. We are thrilled; and now Eleanor has a real grasp of the range of the Goan talent that graces Kenya.

The trip seems to be dissolving any anxieties that Eleanor may have had. She's fallen in love with the country, with everything she's seen and with everyone she's met. The thought of spending the rest of our lives in Kenya now seems like an even more wonderful and plausible idea.

Eleanor and I manage a visit to the Old Port. We select and then haggle with the Muslim trader, over a 9'x6' woven rug and finally settle for a little over ten British pounds (a princely sounding sum in Kenya shillings.)

Later, we squeeze in time for a late afternoon swim at Bamburi Beach. I notice that a large part of that beach that was public before Uhuru, has now been demarcated as the Coast State House for President Kenyatta. Considerable construction is underway to extend the facilities and provide for ancillary accommodations, including security barracks that will be needed. We take a quick look over Kikambala and return to Nyali.

The next day, we set off early for our return journey to Nairobi. We make a stop at Kibwezi for petrol and, for Eleanor, a washroom break. She returns and sits on a picnic bench under the shade of a *makuti-*(palm thatch) lean-to. I tip the African pump attendant and am walking over to join Eleanor, when I notice the young, handsome Goan owner walking toward us.

"Hello, Lando," he says. "Do you remember me from Dr. Ribeiro's Goan School?"

"Of course! Lewis! You haven't changed a bit. It's so good to see you. This is my wife, Eleanor… and as you may or may not have noticed, we are expecting our first child."

Lewis offers Eleanor warm congratulations, and then a hearty pat on the back for me. He then excuses himself with this request: "Can you please stay a minute? I promise, I'll return right away."

Eleanor and I are a bit puzzled but we agree and settle down on the bench together to enjoy the tranquility.

Good as his word, Lewis returns, but not empty handed. He brings a tray bearing three cokes, a large plate of homemade samosas and a dish of succulent sliced mango which he places on the picnic table. He invites us to join him in this generous flash picnic.

"Oh Lewis, this is so kind of you," we both gush. However, while Eleanor is moved by the gesture, I'm a bit concerned that her pregnancy aversion to mango might create an uncomfortable ending to this lovely feast.

I needn't have worried. Those early pregnancy issues were clearly in the past, just as my mother had assured me, and Eleanor was once again (thankfully) a fan of mango.

While we eat, Lewis tells us how he came to be the proprietor of this petrol station.

"My father was working at a nearby sisal farm, but was getting ready to retire and return to Goa. I was hoping to save enough money to go to England to study mechanical engineering at a college; but I was advised by some European friends that I should instead consider joining the British Royal Engineers as a cadet. They would train me in Mechanical Engineering, for free. My mother however, was very nervous about me going to England for any reason. She was worried that I would end up marrying a British girl and disappear forever." (Of course, that scenario was all too familiar to me.)

"So what made you change your mind?" Now, I'm really curious.

"Well, my mum and dad decided to take me to Mombasa on holiday. While there, Dad and I went off alone to fish. We were out there drifting in the boat and he began to talk to me about what I was going to do with my life. I told him about the R.E.M. course. Then he told me that he had been offered this petrol station at a good price and the oil company was keen for him to take it over. What he told me next, changed my life. He said he wanted to buy it so that he and I could own it jointly, but that I would run it as my own business. I said yes, we shook hands, and I never looked back."

"Well congratulations. So, how's it going?"

"It's going great. In my first month, I increased sales from 4,000 gallons per month to 11,250 gallons!"

"Your mother must be so pleased," Eleanor enthuses.

"Between you and me," Lewis says, "I think the trip to Mombasa and the petrol station were her ideas in the first place, and Dad was just the messenger."

"Lesson learned, my friend," I declare.

Eleanor adds with a grin. "Yes, indeed. Women don't mess around when they want something done."

21

Working Wanderlust

July, 1967.

While Eleanor was busy between work and preparing for the arrival of the baby, I was still pondering alternatives for my career. I reflected on Graham's decision to cut his roots in the Kenya he loved and where he had built up an enviable architectural practice. He had provided a good life for his family, and yet he was willing to give it up. He would soon move to the Seychelles to supervise the construction of the Mahe Beach Hotel, financed by a Saudi billionaire.

Meanwhile, I was haunted by an idea that kept echoing in my head. *'Graham is looking after his family very well. Why shouldn't I be free to look after mine just as well?'*

I know, instinctively, I can direct my destiny better and reflect on my family's priorities, if I have the time and freedom to think. I can't expect to find that time or freedom if I'm tethered to someone else's wagon and dependent on someone else's payroll.

I finally make two decisions. The first is to move forward professionally, on my own. The second is that it would be wiser to tell Eleanor after I've worked out the details.

I invite Graham out to lunch. I thank him for the opportunities he's given me. I express how grateful I am for the work we accomplished together and the trust he placed in me. I explain that I want to change direction for myself, and must… for my family. As for the office, I assure him, it's a perfect time for me to make this move since most major projects I've been handling are either completed or at a convenient handover stage. Thankfully, he understands and agrees.

I officially tender my resignation.

As I drive home that evening, it feels like a load has been lifted from my head. I was carrying the onerous weight of indecision. I feel like a free man. I will initially work from home, so that henceforth, my time will be my own.

Now I can tell Eleanor that I've made the momentous decision to redirect our destiny… and knowing her as I do, as someone who has never been afraid of new adventures, I'm sure she'll be excited for us.

"Are you out of your mind?" she wails.

Eleanor is panic-stricken over the news. "The baby is due in less than three months. Exactly how do you imagine we're going to cope? How do we pay our bills? Where will we live?"

I realize that in my attempt to shield Eleanor from stress, I also kept her unaware of my own internal anxiety. Her reaction shocks me at first, but I realize there are a few reasons for it besides her fear of possibly being homeless. The weather has been unseasonably hot, without let-up. There's no air-conditioning in our house; and after dark, the windows must be shut tight or the *dudus* (mosquitos and other flying insects) will dive bomb into our home. This means that any hope of a breeze is dashed. So, the overriding conditions on which to break the news were not exactly optimum. I'm now considering that I might have come up with a better time, place and approach to this life altering pronouncement.

"Lando, maybe we should never have come to Kenya. Things are not like this in England. Maybe we should have listened to Mummy and emigrated to New Zealand. This is truly ridiculous!"

She pauses and takes a deep meditative breath. "Okay, okay," she continues, "I realize, we're here and there's no turning back now, so I'm asking you to please sit down and tell me how you believe we're going to manage."

I sit pensively for a moment and then, I say ... "God will look after us. He hasn't let us down so far." The surprisingly scornful look on Eleanor's face is a sign that I should have kept a rein on those words and the fact that her Protestant upbringing leads her to be more than a bit skeptical about us Catholics placing so much responsibility on the Almighty.

I try again.

"My luv, you have to know that while I'm working for someone else, I simply don't have time to think and plan for a better future for us. If I have to lie awake every night mulling things over, then I'm exhausted and useless the next day. I know I can find work, so if we're to live poor, temporarily, let us enjoy the free time we'll have together."

"But we have bills to pay... and we need a second car...

and soon the baby will arrive and..." Eleanor says.

"... Please don't worry, luv. The savings we set aside from our wedding will see us through the next few months. Listen, I have an idea. I'm going to go and talk to my friend Ed. He has two big projects under construction and maybe he needs a helping hand. I don't have his telephone number so I'll have to drive over there. In case I'm late, don't wait up, okay? You need your sleep." I give her a reassuring hug and close the door behind me.

I step out into the darkness and the sound of a million crickets cheering me along. An eager salivating Cloto, ambushes me. I rub his neck, and explain I'm in a hurry. He slinks away. I've clearly hurt his feelings but I'll have to deal with that later. Right now, my mission is to reach Ed and convince him he needs me.

Ed is a Mexican-American architect, commissioned by the Opus Dei Catholic organization which is expanding both Strathmore College for men and Kianda College for women. A few years earlier, when I was saving for a trip to the UK to visit Saboti, I did quite a few hours of drafting for Ed. So I'm pretty sure I can count on him to have some work for me that will, in the short term, put bread on the table.

As I steer the Beetle onto Peponi Road, a surfeit of thoughts begin rushing through my brain:

- 'If I'm to go into business on my own, and expect to make a dent on the design of public low-income housing, I'll need to get organized immediately.

- I'll need to sell myself to potential clients.

- I must get some written references together
- I need to assemble a portfolio of past projects.
- I'll need to have some business cards made up, so I can start introducing myself to the decision-makers at the NHC (National Housing Corporation) and City Hall.
- And, I must spread the word throughout the professional network that I'm available.

The stream of oncoming headlights seems to be getting heavier. I've often driven after dark on this sparsely lit, winding Peponi Rd, but it's generally been in the other direction, going home. Now, it seems the road has stretched. I'm feeling emotionally drained after the less than pleasant exchange with Eleanor.

Maybe I'll nip into Plums Lane and let my parents in on my decision, before they hear it via the Goan gossip network. What I'm really hoping is that they'll take it better than my wife did and then I'll have allies to help me calm the situation with Eleanor.

'Is my Beetle reading my thoughts' I wonder? Because instead of turning on Plums Lane toward my childhood home, I find myself abruptly turning toward the Goan Gymkhana (GG).

Along the way, I see plywood and corrugated tin shacks that now occupy the public land and private vacant lots where vendors used to sell sacks of charcoal and cylinders of cooking gas. Now I notice that some of the shacks even have electricity. Perhaps, while I've been abroad, City Council has suspended or done away with implementing municipal by-laws?

By the entrance to the Parklands Sports Club which is en route to the GG club, the sign on the gate still says 'For Members Only.' but thankfully, the *'Europeans Only'* sign has been removed and their car park seems full.

It's Friday night and there will be a cadre of my old buddies at the GG club, my second home when growing up. Overcome with an overwhelming urge to see my friends again, I let the Beetle continue on to the club. The Portuguese have a word… *'Saudades'* which means a strong emotional longing to be with friends after a lengthy absence.

I delightedly and possibly temporarily abandon my "Ed" mission.

I've not been to the Club since the welcome reception for Eleanor some months before.

* *

I'm glad to see my old buddies: Savio, Gerson, Victor, Felix, Aqui (Aquinas) and Edgar. The beer flows, we catch up on news and everyone claims to be optimistic about the future. According to my friends, Kenya is booming and there are not enough trained candidates to fill all the vacancies. Most of them are employed in government-owned corporations, or teaching, and other professions, while a couple have branched out as self-employed. They've all made the decision to stay in Kenya. I'm now thinking, if only I had brought Eleanor along with me to hear them, I feel certain it would have allayed her worries.

I explain my plan to start out on my own and I'm encouraged and excited by their enthusiasm for my idea and I'm gratified to find that the Goan Gymkhana community still continues in its commitment of support for fellow Goans. They welcome newcomers and shed a tear of regret for those families whose circumstances require that they forsake Kenya and seek their livelihood elsewhere. Their departures leave an emotional void in those left behind, but life must and does go on for those that remain.

I may have changed with all the travel and time away but I will always remember my roots. My identity is still fundamentally Goan.

Nigel's father claimed that travel changes one's perception and I sense that I have undergone an osmotic transformation that takes me into a bigger, more inclusive, multi-racial world.

The bartender barks the much-dreaded words. "Last orders, please."

And in that moment, my friend Aqui presents an offer with a smile. "Lando, come see me Monday morning, I may have a project to get you started. Nine sharp please."

"Thank you, Aqui. I can certainly do with a starter project."

"Good, it's settled then. By the way, what do you plan to call your firm?"

"I haven't even thought of a name yet," I stammer uncomfortably. He's caught me off-guard but I think for a nano-second and then flippantly ask; "What's wrong with my name?"

"*Lando Menezes, Architect?* Why not? It's a good name," he concurs with a pat on the back.

We shake hands and go our separate ways.

As I wend my way home, the thrilling idea that I may have my first client is now raising my confidence and excitement levels to epic heights. Then I remember, that Eleanor thought I had rushed out to see Ed about a job. How do I illuminate serendipity? How do I explain that a visit to Ed morphed into a night of hanging out and drinking with my friends at the club?

I arrive home to my sleeping wife... and like a good husband, I'm very careful not to wake her.

* *

I arise early, leave a note for my sleepy wife, and head off to my 9 A.M. appointment with Aqui at the spanking new headquarters of the Shell Oil Company on Harambee Avenue. The building is set on a shining marble podium. The reception desk is a sparkling slab of polished marble that appears to float in space. I stand in front of the gleaming stainless steel lift. It opens and I enter the cabin which is beautifully panelled in rich red mahogany. I exit on the eighth floor. Immediately ahead are the double glass doors to the Chief Engineer's Office.

The European receptionist-secretary is polite, but adamant. "There is no record of such a meeting in my appointment book," she says. "You may sit there and read the newspaper... then, if and when he is free, perhaps he will come out."

"But, Mr. DeSouza specifically said I should be here at 9 A.M. sharp, as he has a busy day; so could you please at least inform him that I'm here," I politely request.

The lady glances up over the rim of her eyeglasses, but says nothing. Her body language says it all. She officiously shuffles papers back and forth over the glass tabletop ignoring me.

I resign myself to waiting. I glance at the newspaper headlines which are all about more government directives on work permits to be issued and new announcements of foreign aid gifted to Kenya. 'The '*Shifta*' nomadic tribal insurgents from Somalia have carried out more cattle raids across the Kenyan border and on some European owned farms near Laikipia.'

At 9:10 A.M. Aqui barges out of his office and hands the secretary a slip of paper that I recognize as the one on which I scribbled my phone number at the club.

"Please call …" he spots me then turns to his receptionist. "Why didn't you tell me Mr. Menezes is already here?" She throws him a hostile glance, but says nothing.

As Aqui whisks me down to the ground floor, he explains that his lift is one of Nairobi's fastest and most expensive. We walk across the polished marble floor towards the 'floating marble' reception desk. The carefully obscured stainless steel brackets that hold it up, create the illusion that the desk is hovering in space. The elegant glass-enclosed foyer, is raised about two feet above the sidewalk outside.

"Lando, since Shell House was first inaugurated, no receptionist wants to sit at this desk. The pedestrians slow down to gawk at them as they walk past the glass façade. The receptionists feel like they're today's sales specials on display. They're demanding we install a solid courtesy panel along the front of the desk to give them some privacy. Can you design something that will blend in with this design?"

I'm dumbfounded. Could this be the project he had in mind or is he just pulling my leg?

"Five years at University studying interior design and architecture… to design a privacy shield? Do you have a multi-year budget for this?" I sarcastically jest as I adjust my glasses and whisk out a pen and notebook.

"Lando, I know it's a very small job… but yes, that's the project." Aqui says somewhat apologetically. "My problem is, we have our 'retained architects' who do all our company's major work; but frankly I'm embarrassed to give them this small job. Do you think you can handle it? It's a petty cash item, so there's no actual budget for it," he quietly mentions.

No matter what I'm feeling, there's no turning back now. I've just met with my first client.

"Thanks Aqui, since I have no other projects at this time, this is already my biggest so far. We can probably have the panel designed and installed in about two weeks."

He seems pleased. We shake hands and go our separate ways.

I unlock the car, drop a few coins into the outstretched hand of a self-appointed, parking '*toto*' (young boy), steer the Beetle into slow-moving traffic, and head for home. As I drive along, I remember Stephen's now prophetic words after my return from England when he was lamenting over the difficulty in securing employment: *'If you do not have important friends in high places, you cannot get work in Kenya these days.'*

22

Our Wheels of Fortune

When I arrive home, Eleanor is there anxiously waiting to hear news about my meeting last night with "Ed."

I confess that I'd felt compelled to turn away from my intended goal to meet with Ed and had instead driven toward the club… "And my darling, what a karmic decision it turned out to be. My friend, Aqui has been promoted to Chief Engineer for Shell. He's been with them for years and he's damn good, but could never get promoted before Uhuru. Now finally, a Kikuyu has been appointed as CEO. Some European managers have taken their pensions and moved on. Africans and brown Kenyan citizens have been promoted. But today, most important to us is that he has a project for me."

Eleanor breathed a sigh of relief to hear that I had secured a job; therefore I wasn't going to complain to her about the type of job it was or how brief the employment might be.

* *

A few days later while in town, I bump into Angelo Faria, a prominent Goan economist who has chosen to remain in Kenya. We manage to grab seats in the Beer Garden of the Norfolk Hotel. We talk about the assassination of Pio Gama

Pinto, the Goan Member of Parliament; and he confirms the rumour of a heated argument between President Mzee Jomo Kenyatta and Gama Pinto the day before his death.

"I wish Fritz DeSouza (one of Kenyatta's young lawyers at the Kapenguria trial) would speak. He must know something. They were very close friends."

"Anyway, Lando, enough of politics. How's married life?"

"Wonderful," I reply. "How about you? Have you taken the plunge?"

"Staying single while I figure out my future plans," he says. "There's stiff competition for housing since the lifting of racial residential segregation and the additional pressures from the thousands of *Wageni* willing to pay higher rents."

"Yes, I've learned firsthand that the cost of housing is a killer. The only affordable accommodation is on the fringes of the city. We managed to find a small place near Kitisuru. Now, with Eleanor expecting a baby, security and transportation are our two biggest problems."

We are momentarily distracted by a young European man in a bright floral shirt and khaki safari jacket who brusquely treks past us toward the bar. He pauses briefly to scan the crowd, then perches himself on a stool, orders a beer and sits gazing out at the street. Angelo and I resume our conversation.

"You were saying something about transportation?" Angelo reminds me.

"Oh yes, thanks. Sure, when the baby comes, we must have a second car. With all the security problems on Peponi

Road, we can't have a jalopy that might break down. The trouble is we're broke right now, so a jalopy is about all we can afford."

"How do you manage without a car now?"

"Most of the time, she drives in with me, drops me off and takes the Beetle to her workplace. If our schedules don't match and I need to leave earlier, then I take the car and she takes a ride in with our neighbour."

With that thought fresh on my lips, I glance at my watch. "Oh wow, speaking of my wife, I have to go. She's at home today, she had a free day from work. But I parked my car at my parent's house and walked here."

Angelo offers up a whistle. "That's a hell of a walk, Lando."

"It's a good walk. About thirty minutes of time I use to clear my head. Anyway, I need to get back, pick up the car and head home in case Eleanor needs to do some shopping before dark. See? If we had two cars, it would solve that problem."

"Have you checked with Mechanic Lobo? He may be able to find you a good deal."

"Yes, thanks, that's what I have planned to do this weekend."

We drink up, say goodbye and I walk under the brick arch to head off toward Plums Lane. As I'm about to cross the street, I spot a Volkswagen Kombi parked at the curb. It intrigues me. It has a black roof rack, a creamy white top with a warm somewhat faded tomato red chassis. A route map is painted across the body on all sides; Key cities are printed in black. The journey begins at the front right fender in London, the English Channel transverses the grill, then moves along the left fender to France, continues on to the driver's door to Spain, the rear door to Germany, and follows on to every single part of the van… through the Eastern Bloc countries, and on through to Istanbul in Turkey where Eleanor and I went on our European Safari. The route circles the van once again; south along the Turkish Coast, zig-zags a bit to restart in Alexandria in Egypt and overland across Africa, to Cape Town. A green line starts the return trip in Cape Town, up the Garden Route, through Swaziland, Mozambique, and Tanzania and seems to break into a dotted line from Tanga to Mombasa, a slight diversion to Arusha, and back to Kenya. It stops firmly in Nairobi at the rear right fender.

I'm curious and excited. What a trip that must have been! I was so mesmerized by the journey, I hadn't noticed the sheet of paper pasted on the windshield with a crudely hand-written message that reads 'FOR IMMEDIATE SALE (AS IS). PLEASE ASK AT HOTEL BAR BEFORE 6:30 P.M.'

I glance at my watch. It's 6:18 P.M. I rush back to the bar. The man in the floral shirt and safari khakis, I'd noticed earlier, slips off the barstool and approaches me. He's in his mid-twenties, heavily sunburned with ginger hair that glows like a neon sign.

He offers me a handshake. "I take it, you're curious about the van?" he inquires in an unmistakable English accent.

Of course the question puzzles me. How did he know?

"Oh, believe me, I wasn't stalking you, I was just watching

you checking it out. I'm Bill, and yes, I'm selling the van." he confirms. "And I suppose you will want to know why?"

I smile weakly and nod.

He explains that he and his two friends made the trip to Cape Town from the UK, as shown on the route map. However, on the return journey they hit bad luck. Freedom fighters in Mozambique robbed them of their cash and belongings, but let them go with their lives. The trio was able to replenish some of the missing items in Lorenco Marques, but bad luck struck again with a mechanical problem in Tanzania which was fixed with the help of a crackerjack Sikh mechanic. As if that wasn't enough trauma, Charles, one of the travelers developed a serious infection that led to complications that could not be fixed by the Sikh mechanic. In fact, Bill's friend Thomas was instructed by a Greek doctor in Arusha to get Charles to a hospital in London immediately. It was decided that Thomas would accompany the patient to the UK and Bill would be entrusted to sell the Kombi and return to London as soon as it was done.

Bill assures me, "the vehicle runs beautifully." He's asking for ninety-five British pounds, payable in Kenya shillings, which is a pittance. I'm moved by his story and under better circumstances, if I were to buy it, I might have offered him more money than he was asking. The fact that I desperately need a second car and his word that 'the vehicle runs' would have been enough to inspire me to make the sale; but then a thought hit me. What if the vehicle was stolen? Since Independence, Kenya has been attracting con-men, and they come in all colours.

"I will need proper papers to license the vehicle," I insist.

"I have all the papers," he says, "If you're interested you can give me a ten percent deposit now to confirm your commitment, and we can meet tomorrow and do the paperwork at the motor vehicle licensing office."

"I have absolutely no cash on me, so I'll need to get to my parents' home on Plums Lane to get you your deposit. It's not far," I say reassuringly. "But it will take me about forty minutes to walk there, get the money and drive back here. He looks at me, quizzically. I imagine he's thinking, I'm the con-man who he just saw spend my last pennies of savings on a beer.

I ask. "Are you a guest at this hotel?"

"No, I am actually staying at the Mayfair Hotel on Waiyaki Road. Listen, if it will help, I can take you to Plums Lane. I know where it is. It's by the Parklands Sports Club, right? And you could test-drive the van. The best time to do it is before you pay." He hands me the key. I accept.

As we pass the Goan Gymkhana club, I begin to hope that my Dad will still be at his card game so I won't have to face his resistance to what I'm sure he'll deem to be an irresponsible decision.

We arrive at Plums Lane where I find Mum to be eagerly obliging as she readily hands me the money. "I must say, Lando, you are lucky that Dad is still at the Club," she smiles, "I'm sure you can imagine what he would have to say about this."

"That's why I came directly to you, Mum." I chuckle as I

enfold her in a bear hug.

As I release her, my mum turns to Bill and invites him to stay for dinner.

"Oh, I'm so grateful for the invitation." He begins, "I love Goan food. I have Goan neighbours in London on Hayes Rd. who often invite me to share a meal with them and it's always a delicious pleasure. But unfortunately, I must decline. I have so much to take care of before I leave tomorrow. But thank you so much for your kindness which I find typical of the Goan People I've met."

The deal is made and Bill and I arrange to meet at the same spot outside the Norfolk hotel, the next morning to take care of the details.

* *

I arrive home to share all the news with Eleanor. I assure her that the Kombi runs perfectly well, in spite of the amazing overland journey it's been through. "Listen my luv, if it doesn't work out, we can sell it to a scrap dealer and still get more than we paid for it."

She responds with one of her endearing giggles and once again, all is right in my world.

* *

The next evening, as I turn into our driveway with our new old van, Stephen rushes over, ecstatic. "You must remove this back seat, Bwana Lando; so we can take the vegetables to the market."

I'm amused at his optimism since no soil has been turned nor has he laid out any planting beds as yet.

Early the next morning, under Cloto's supervision, we remove the back seat and Stephen gives the car a good wash. Eleanor watches in amusement. "Finding this car for so little money, was a complete stroke of luck," she muses. "We must call it, our wheels of fortune."

August, 1967.

My plans to start up my own practice are underway. I rush about setting up an office at home. At most I will have about two months to work in our second bedroom before its precious and rightful resident evicts me. I buy a typewriter, order stationary, a drafting board and a filing cabinet. As a precautionary measure to ensure I can pay the bills until my name becomes known, I sign a contract to help my architect friend, Ed, with his projects at Strathmore College and Kianda College.

23

The Birth of a New Day

October 29, 1967

I leave the warm hospital and head into the cold night. As I walk to the car park I reflect on the false labour alarms we've been through and I consider this is likely to be another, which leads me to feeling grateful to Eleanor and the medical staff for insisting I go home and get some rest. But I can't help but wonder if the real reason they're anxious to see me off is that Eleanor will rest so much better without me watching the clock, pacing nervously and asking repeatedly, 'do you think it's for real this time?'

It's well after 1 A.M. as I drive out of the hospital car park, through the city centre, across to the Westlands intersection with Waiyaki Road, past the AGIP petrol station towards Peponi Road. It's always at this point on the route that I notice the night getting blacker. Perhaps it's just that City Council no longer replaces burnt-out streetlamps.

In the bends and turns along the winding road, I begin to imagine I'm seeing vans parked in the shadows. Then I'm sure I hear a car gaining on me. I accelerate. In my rear view mirror the headlights get closer and the engine roar's louder. Suddenly there's an insistent honking beside me before the car quickly overtakes me, swerving dangerously close. It races away into the darkness while I'm left to calm my shattered nerves and drive on.

The glow from the stars on a clear night guides me along the dark silent road to home. Cloto, bounds toward the car with his usual eager welcome dance. I stop by the front entrance, inhale the cold crisp night air and gaze across the valley to Kitisuru.

The crickets and tree frogs are awake and vocalizing in unison. In the distance I hear a dog bark. I feel comforted by Cloto as he nuzzles resolutely and heavily against my shins.

"You'll have to be gentler than this when the baby arrives, Cloto." I stroke his head and run my hand along the ridge of his strong back. I explain that I left Eleanor at the maternity ward in the hope we'll soon bring home our baby. He casually turns around and slouches back to his kennel.

I let myself into the house by the kitchen entrance, then I latch and lock both sections of the stable-doors. An increase in burglaries on Peponi Road has made us all more diligent.

The empty house feels eerie. I can't help but dwell on what the neighbour told us about our house having been raided three times by panga (machete) wielding gangs. The thought drives me to wonder again about those vans I imagined I saw in the shadows.

With large flows of foreign money suddenly entering Kenya after Independence, newspapers have reported that in the city there has been a rise in violent crimes. Some say, the police are under-funded, others claim the police don't care.

'Does anyone care anymore?' With that cynical question racing through my head, I undress, flop into bed and fall fast asleep.

In my sleep, I imagine I hear Cloto barking, but it's only a dream and I continue to sleep soundly until I'm suddenly awakened, by an orange glow of moving light. Someone is shining a flashlight through the Jinja Cotton curtains.

My heart is pulsating. I'm in bed facing a three-paneled window that is secured with metal-mesh burglar-proofing, but I know there's an intruder out there. Or is it more than one? I quietly slide out of bed and reach for a *rungu*, a heavy wooden stick with a gnarled, lumpy knob that I can use as a weapon. My eye is slowly drawn to a fist-sized hole in the metal-mesh where someone has undoubtedly breached the screen with clippers. The next thing I see is an extended hand clutching a bamboo pole with a metal hook attached and guiding it through the window. I bend low and tiptoe to the wall and stand to the right of the window frame. I raise my *weapon* and slam it down on the unsuspecting wrist. The intruder screams like a banshee and instantly drops the pole and flashlight. The scream subsides as the footsteps on gravel begin to fade. But now I can hear someone trying to break through the stable door.

I rush from room to room, turning on lights and shouting instructions as if there was a throng of people inside. Any weekday, Stephen would have been in his quarters, but on weekends he goes home to his mother's village. I'm alone.

I stop briefly to listen. I hear another set of footsteps on the gravel but they're fading. Seconds pass like hours. Finally, I hear only the loud thumping of my heart, and then a beautiful comforting silence.

I return to bed, certain that I will not sleep but at 4:25 A.M. I'm awakened by the ringing phone. As I turn on the light, it stops. I roll over. It rings again, seemingly louder than an alarm.

It's the duty nurse at the hospital.

"Mr. Menezes, the baby decided to arrive not too long after you left. It was very fast. So, congratulations! You are the father of a lovely baby girl! Eleanor is fine and resting. Baby is fine; and I've been asked to insist that you get some sleep and come by later in the morning."

I thank her and hang up. I'm left stunned, delighted and… in a quandary. My heart tells me I should brave the night and go, but my instinct tells me it would be unwise to venture into that foreboding night again. I know what Eleanor would advise me to do. So as telepathically advised, I wait for daybreak.

At this point, sleep is hopeless. I brew a pot of coffee and write to my in-laws in England announcing the arrival of their first grandchild.

At 5:50 A.M. I hear the first excited chirping of birds. Perhaps they heard the news of our new baby from the hospital pigeon telegraph.

I go out to feed Cloto and find him slumped by the side of

the house. He's alive, but barely. His eyes are open and there is life in them. It's clear the offenders tranquilized him to prevent him from incessantly barking. It's a Sunday morning and I don't know where I'll find a vet. I bring Cloto a large bowl of water. He laps at a few drops, I stroke his head and neck and run my fingers over his back. I tell him I'm going to see Eleanor and our new baby and I will come straight back to look after him. He manages to wag his short tail with enough verve to let me know he understands.

* *

At the information desk, I'm directed to Room N-34. I knock gently and open the door. The bed is empty. I peek into the crib and find a beautiful tan-coloured baby wrapped in blue. His big, dark sparkling eyes are staring back at me.

I return to the corridor and take a second look at the nameplate: Room N-34: Mutiso/Menezes.

A lady's voice calls out. "Hello Lando, are you looking for Eleanor?"

It is Flora Mutiso, the wife of a professional colleague of mine who sits on the Board of the Architectural Association of Kenya with me. "Did you check behind the partition? She should be there. You have a most beautiful baby girl."

"Thank you. Your handsome little chap just inspected me," I said. "I hope I didn't traumatize him. What's his name?"

"Kenya," Flora says. "Kenya Mutiso."

"A good name," I admit as I offer my congratulations.

I enter the room and peek behind the curtain. Eleanor and our daughter are radiant... and both sleeping soundly.

Flora whispers, "It was a long night for her... maybe they could use another few hours of rest."

I tell Flora what happened and about my concern for Cloto and ask that she tell my wife only that I was here and will be back soon. I impress upon her that I need to tell Eleanor about this incident myself so as not to frighten her. She agrees.

I head home to check on Cloto. I see that he had vomited behind his kennel but thankfully, he drank all the water and was much improved. A smaller dog would never have made it. But Cloto is over the worst. I put out a mix of *Ugali* (corn meal) and meat, top up his water and return to the hospital.

During the course of the day, the baby is still tired from her big entrance and sleeps like a princess while Eleanor anxiously recounts for me the experience of her first birth.

"After you left, a nurse gave me an enema and stuck me in an empty room with a bell to ring if the pains got really bad. Then I lay there alone in the dark."

"How bad do the pains have to get? Who decides when they're bad enough?"

"Oh, they got really bad and then even worse. I thought I can't stand this till the morning, so I rang the bell."

"You weren't in the delivery room at this point?"

"No. The nurse came, took a cursory look at me and shrieked 'oh my God, the baby's crowning.' She rushed me into the delivery room. Our baby was born around 2.00 A.M. and Sister Amin, a lovely Indian girl, washed her and put her in my arms. I was amazed by this little one's beauty, her shock of long dark hair, her fine features and the dimple in her chin, which she likely inherited from me... or my father."

"Hang on. Let me take a closer look and I'll tell you." I inspect every inch of the baby's precious face and then walk over to my wife's bed and closely inspect her chin. I give her a gentle kiss on the dimple and cheekily conclude: "The dimple's definitely inherited from you."

"Okay, darling, enough about me, how was your night?"

I carefully drip-feed Eleanor with select details of my night. She is shocked but relieved it's over.

The next day it's reported that two vicious panga gang robberies along Peponi Road had occurred in the early hours of the previous morning. The intrusion at our home, had it not been aborted, would have been the third attack. I feel a shiver up my spine at the thought of the unimaginable consequences for Eleanor and our new baby had they been home. I definitely do not share those horrifying thoughts with Eleanor who is safely immune from the news in the quiet isolation of her hospital bed.

Over the next three days Eleanor describes each day in hospital as the best time of her life. Friends come bearing gifts and flowers. She sleeps from 11 P.M. to 5 A.M. She's happy to go along with the hospital policy of keeping the babies in the nursery overnight to allow the mothers to get their much needed rest.

Four days later, Eleanor and baby are en route to a warm welcome from Stephen, Cloto and Mary, an ayah highly recommended by one of our friends.

As we drive along the road toward home, Nairobi seems

particularly alive and beautiful. The rains brought out the flowers and scents of greenery on wet earth. The bright red flamboyant also in bloom, form a canopy along the driveway.

When we arrive, Eleanor settles into a wingchair in the garden, feeding our beautiful daughter while I take photographs from every angle.

"Let's call her 'Alice Emily,'" Eleanor excitedly suggests. "Alice, after your Mum and Emily, for herself."

"Alice in our Kenyan Wonderland! Brilliant. Yes, let's call her Alice."

I make her a 'cuppa' and sit beside her.

Yellow-breasted weaverbirds cheerfully chatter in and out of the branches of the two old jacaranda trees in fullest bluest bloom. A shower of rain during the night delivered a fresh carpet of petals in violets and blues.

24

Getting Down to Business

October 3, 1967

Within weeks of starting my business at home, Eleanor served me with an eviction notice. "Luv, the baby's due in three weeks, so I'll need you to start using the dining table for your drawing board?"

* *

A chance meeting with Ed Hernandez's landlord in Solar House turns out to be a lucky break for me. I tell him I'm starting out on my own and I'm seeking advice on where to find cheap office space. He convinces me to consider leasing a 'shop' on the upper floor of a pedestrian arcade in his building. It's been vacant for at least a year. Maybe that's because it's at the dead end of the arcade. I decide that it's not a liability to me. I figure I can turn it into a nice private lunch terrace for my future staff.

Mr. Patel offers me the space rent-free for the first two months, but requires that I deliver a *Letter of Credit* from my Bank within sixty days. By the end of the week my home office is relocated to Solar House.

I embark on my first attempt at writing short fiction – 'a business plan.' I must estimate an income, have an operating budget to secure a source and constant flow of funding until the work-stream expands. I must also plan for a secretary and a draughtsman. I make an appointment to meet the manager at the Barclays Bank branch next door.

A rather stern-looking British manager, Mr. Davidson, is seated behind a large sleek desk looking rather like a diner, seated at a restaurant table, awaiting service. Two In/Out paper trays, a polished brass pencil holder, a sparkling gold pen on a stand, and a flip-card calendar advertising forthcoming races at the Ngong Race Track are the only trappings on the desk.

"How can I help you?" he asks politely.

I hand him my business plan. I had also rehearsed an impressive script for the occasion, but I can't afford to lose his trust. I need his help, so I toss the script from my mind and instead confess my dire situation.

I tell him:

"My wife is expecting our first baby.

We own an old VW Kombi, which is fully paid up.

We have a new VW Beetle, which is being paid for in instalments.

We have only two domestic helpers, Stephen who is already with us, and an Ayah, Mary, who will arrive with the baby."

He casts a cursory glance at the Business Plan and appears unmoved.

I continue:

"We own a home on three acres of land on a former coffee estate.

Here are two promissory notes and a mortgage document."

He smiles for the first time, "Do you intend to consolidate these loans in a traditional mortgage?" he asks.

I politely offer a firm, "No, Sir." His smile disappears. He asks about my income.

I tell him I have just finished a respected project for Shell at their headquarters on Harambee Avenue. He methodically removes a notepad and ball point pen from his desk drawer and curtly scribbles something.

I don't mention that it was merely a 'courtesy panel' for the reception counter.

"I'm about to start on another notable project for this same client," I say. I show him photographs of some of my other completed projects. His face is inscrutable. I fear he is about to show me the door. My heart is pounding in my head until suddenly I begin to realise, I have nothing to lose if I show him all my cards. I place on his desk a folder of newspaper cuttings from the *East African Standard* and the *Daily Nation, March 1963*, when I received the award for the design competition for the Independence celebrations. There is the Minister of Works shaking my hand; and looking on, Amyas Connell, Royal Gold Medalist of the R.I.B.A, and current President of the Architectural Association of Kenya. As he scratches another note to himself, he suddenly appears annoyed. He angrily throws the ballpoint pen into the wastepaper basket, then reaches for the gold *Parker 51* ink pen on his desk and carefully writes a note.

I sense the interview is over for me. I'm now quietly seething. I should have followed the somewhat fictionalized scripted story I'd concocted, instead of opening my heart to this blood-sucking Imperial sadist. He looks up.

"Why did you choose Barclays Bank and not the National Bank of India?"

"Because I have rented office space next door in Solar House. Also my dad works at the National Bank. He's already lent me his own money and since he doesn't believe in people living beyond their means, it would embarrass him to see me begging."

"As a rule, your dad is right, in as far as one's domestic life is concerned. However as I understand it, you want to borrow money to finance your architectural and urban planning consulting practice. You need this loan to earn the money needed to feed your family, employ others in the future, and to pay salaries and bills. Correct?"

"Exactly sir. That's why I'm here." This man is talking down to me, and I'm pretending to be impressed. I think I may have cracked this nut.

"Here's what we'll do. We will open an account and I will place a limit on what you can draw each month. For the first few months, you must bring me a statement of exactly what bills you must pay, the actual income received and a separate list of expected fees receivable for the next ninety days. That's what banks are here for, young man."

I offer thanks in return. He rises and peers through the

glass partition. He signals to one of the Kenyan underlings. I stand and we shake hands.

The young Kenyan assistant enters. I accompany him to his cubicle to complete the paperwork.

I'm now in business under my own name. Within two weeks I'm organized in my new office space, (it beats the dining table,) with some basic furniture, two drafting boards, paper supplies, a brief case, office stationary and a very sharp business card.

* *

October 22, 1967

About a week before the baby's due, I'm summoned to a meeting with the Chief Engineer's staff at Shell House. I'm really excited about the project, as it is my first 'return' client. Aqui De Souza presides for the opening remarks. "After we read your preliminary report, we have had internal discussions and decided that the Mvita Shell Station in Mombasa will be completely renovated by your company," Aqui says.

The Oil Company places some preconditions on my contract. First, that I will be solely and completely responsible for the design and construction supervision from start to finish and that the official 'retained architects' will not oversee this project. Second, the entire underground infrastructure will also be replaced. Third, since the Mombasa station is one of their busiest outlets, under no circumstances can it be completely shut down at any time during construction.

We agree that the Engineers Department will provide whatever records and plans exist, and meanwhile it will commission a more detailed 'age and condition' study of the technical infrastructure. Albeit small and messy, I know this will be an interesting and challenging project.

The Shell Mvita Station on Mombasa Island is the oldest petrol station, built by the then Burmah Oil, in Kenya in 1902. It is located on a busy road connecting with the mainland over the Makupa Bridge. Both the road and the station are congested with cars, trucks, and motorbikes, as well as bicycles and pedestrians. A Swahili neighbourhood of tiny coral-block houses, roofed with *makuti* (palm thatch) or with flattened rusty *debes* (cans) surrounds it on three sides. Prior to the advent of steam and later diesel-powered ships, dhows from India and the Gulf States, transported an interesting range of commodities in sealed four-gallon (1 UK gallon = 4.5litres) rectangular cans. These empty cans when flattened found yet another use as roofing material.

When the station was originally built at the turn of the Twentieth Century, diesel oil and petrol was pumped right out of forty-gallon drums and straight into vehicles or portable containers. Kerosene, also pumped by hand, was transported in rectangular four-gallon debes carried on dhows to the Old Port of Mombasa, where shipments of poor quality rugs arrived from the Gulf States. Then the dhows sailed away again with a cargo of mangrove poles, raw coconuts, and many other exotic local products.

This job is my first big break! I realise that my reputation and future income depends on it. I become obsessive. I study the company's OM (Operational Manual) which dictates the design specifications - the minutiae for guiding its operatives around the planet were dreamed up by marketing moguls and engineers in some distant land. I learn that *'Brand and Image'* is everything in marketing, so I vow that my firm will evolve its own brand and image and my designs will be attractive, functional and environmentally sensitive to their surroundings.

* *

October 29, 1969

As I intimated at the very beginning of this story, that was *the night of all nights,* because that was the night that a bowl of Jeanette's hot and sour soup helped to hurry our first born into this fascinating and sometimes scary world.

It left us with our beautiful baby Alice and a whole lot of stories we can tell her… when she's old enough to handle 'The Mysteries on Peponi Road.'

But for now, we're just basking in the innocent warm glow of parenthood.

* *

Mid-November, 1967

I'm requested to appear for an interview with the Chief Architect at the National Housing Corporation (NHC). He questions me on my overall experience on contract supervision and then whisks me away to meet his boss, an impressive professorial gentleman, whom I recognise as being from Western Kenya. He is not a Kikuyu.

After a brief introduction, he explains that Britain's policy of placing restrictions on the free movement of its nationals is causing havoc with the work program of his Corporation. I glance toward the Chief Architect, a British expatriate who stands transfixed and staring out a window. He seems uncomfortable but says nothing. Perhaps he's trying to catch a glimpse of Mt. Kilimanjaro, a hundred and fifty miles in the distance. Maybe he'd prefer to be on its peak looking down at us through binoculars rather than listening to this CEO waxing 'eloquent.'

"We have embarked on a major project to increase the supply of housing for mid-level civil servants in the Woodley area," the CEO continues. "Kenyans in an Independent Kenya want to live like Mzungus. They will not accept living in the old Indian Quarters that were previously provided to Goan civil servants in Ngara. I understand you are from Goa. I have many Goan friends from my teaching days in Kisumu."

I'm not sure where he is going, so I do not comment. He continues. "So let me tell you why we have asked you here. About two weeks ago, the Indian in-house architect who was on our permanent staff suddenly quit his job and left for the UK. I understand his Entry Visa was approved so that he could take his family with him. Meanwhile the contractor has continued working here without any technical supervision. The Corporation wishes that you will accept the contract to supervise the work to completion." The interview ends.

The Chief Architect, having joined us finally in spirit, leads me to his office where I am presented with a technical package that includes: a Bill of Quantities and a draft Standard Contract with fees as prescribed by the Architectural

Association of Kenya. A few days later I have a signed contract. I arrange for a first site meeting with the Contractor. The fees for the period of construction do not amount to much, but it will reassure my bank that I am bringing work in. It also allows me to hire secretarial temp services, and start thinking of employing a draftsman.

* *

On the weekend, Eleanor complains of 'cabin fever' and suggests we take the baby for a ride up to the Ngong Hills. It's a beautiful Sunday afternoon and as we are returning home, I decide to show Eleanor the Woodley site. The *Askari*, (Security Guard) pleased to have company turn up in this lonely isolated site, quickly opens the gate for us.

I park the Beetle under the shade of a tree in a somewhat secluded corner of the parking lot for privacy. Eleanor remains inside to breastfeed Alice.

I clamber over half-dug trenches towards the few of the buildings where the foundations are at plinth level. I notice that the damp-proof course, a waterproofing membrane required by the building code, is missing from most of the units already out of the ground.

As I make notes, I'm interrupted by the exasperating sound of my Beetle's croaky horn beeping relentlessly. The security guard hears it too. We both rush towards the car. I can see Eleanor inside the car waving her red scarf. As we get closer, I can see that she is pointing to a black line in front of the car. It looks like a settlement crack in the tarmac surface. On second glance, I realise it's not a crack. It's a six-foot snake just lying there resting or waiting there between the car and me. At first I think I might scare it away by throwing rocks in its direction, but if it has young ones nearby, it could get very nervous which makes me extremely nervous. Eleanor in the meantime is already past nervous with her own young one in the car. Fear aside, she manages to start the engine. The noise persuades the snake to slither away into the long grass. This has been Eleanor's first, up-close and personal encounter with 'Kenyan wildlife'.

**

Two days later, I'm at my first site meeting. I tell the Contractor that I can foresee many accidents waiting to happen to his labour because of the way things are being mishandled. I instruct him to demolish all the walls down to the plinth level. I can see the shock on his face. I inform him that I will personally inspect the demolition, and I expect to see far better management of the site. He nervously agrees to rebuild the Units correctly as required in the specifications.

They next day, my friend Mengha Singh, a contractor, walks into my office grinning broadly. Apparently the word of my direct instructions to the Woodley contractor, to demolish the walls, had spread through the contractor fraternity like a bush-fire.

"You now have a reputation as an *mbwa kali* (very strict) architect who will not tolerate any nonsense."

"Great! I can live with that," I firmly reply.

25

Preparing for Christmas

Life on the domestic front is settling into a routine of sorts. Eleanor is occupied with the baby. And with her now sole use of the Beetle, she is driving regularly to visit friends, to Plums Lane to share the baby with Mum, or off to see my sister Fatima in Westlands. Fatima has a ton of experience with her bevy of three beautiful little girls aged three and two years, and the baby only six months old.

One evening I return home, to find my wife bubbling with excitement. "Guess who came to visit today?" she says. "Flora Mutiso. She brought little Kenya over. You wouldn't mistake him for our daughter now, Lando. As a boy should, he's put on more weight than our little Alice. He looks so cute with his big eyes and adorable smile."

"Did she see changes in Alice?"

"Yes, of course. She commented on her dimples, her weight gain, her adorable cooing. I loved having them here. She stayed for lunch and we chatted a lot."

"Not about Kenya politics, I hope?"

"No, just family stories. Did you know that she and David were both born in Kangundo, Machakos? Isn't that where our friends Don and Pam are farming? I didn't know this earlier, but Flora is a Registered Midwife in the United Kingdom, and a Registered Nurse in England &Wales, Scotland and Kenya."

"Maybe that's why she seemed so relaxed when you were both in the maternity ward together. Without trying, she was calming me down whenever I came by to see you. So Luv, I'm curious... did they meet and marry in Machakos?"

"No, they met at a Mkamba Reverend's residence in the UK. He was hosting a party for the Wakamba members of the Legislative Council attending the Lancaster House Conference to negotiate for Kenya's Independence. The two were invited separately."

"I thought David studied architecture at the University of Sheffield?"

"Yes, he did, and then he went to Nottingham for his Town Planning Diploma. They were married in the Church of St. George the Martyr, Queens Square, Holborn, London."

"You should be working for the C.I.D (Criminal Investigation Department)," I quip, "'cause you learned an awful lot in such a short time."

"Not so short. Flora just left at tea time," Eleanor says. "But it was so much fun. We agreed to try and meet at least once a month, to compare notes. She loves Alice, and hopes their next child will be a girl."

* *

Stephen is making progress with his projects. About a week after Alice's arrival, he returns from a shopping trip at the open market at Westlands. He's carrying a cane cage packed with three live hens and a cock. On the 25th of November he delivers the first two freshly laid eggs to the kitchen. He announces that we can expect at least two eggs daily, and when the third hen is ready, there will three eggs. His vegetable garden is also taking shape. In addition, he delivers fresh cut flowers to Eleanor on demand as promised. It's a proud day for him.

On the weekend, we visit the BOMBAX Nursery at Dagoretti Corner to purchase new seedlings. Stephen now struts around the property with a newfound confidence. He seems to be overcoming the terrible trauma of his childhood in detention. He has befriended an older more experienced gardener at our neighbour's property. Eleanor and I are constantly looking for hints or clues in Steven's behaviour that might lead to better vocational training for him.

Mary, the ayah, has established a routine for the baby and Eleanor. She comes with much experience handling Mzungu and Wahindi babies. Each day, Mary takes Alice from Eleanor after her first feed. She washes and dresses her, then takes her out to enjoy the gentle morning sunshine. That's when I usually greet Alice before I leave for work. Most days, she's asleep by the time I reach home.

I'm sitting on the patio, on this almost perfect morning, amidst the happy chattering of weaverbirds when Alice, in Mary's arms, greets me with a broad smile.

"Good morning, Alice my sweet. Good morning, Mary. I haven't seen Cloto up and around yet. Have you seen Stephen?" I ask. She points to the end of the driveway. I stand

and spot Cloto and see that Steven is interacting with a group of panga -wielding women. I grab my jacket and brief case, and drive up to Stephen.

"Good morning Bwana Lando," he greets me cheerfully. "My sister-friends are waiting for you."

This moment requires some explanation. Bear with me.

We are the most isolated of all our neighbours on Peponi Road. Beyond us, the coffee plantations are still in production, although new subdivisions are rumoured to be encroaching on productive coffee land around Nairobi, like some non-curable creeping disease. We hear of the existence of a *Settlement Village*' somewhere beyond the coffee fields, but we dare not go there. It's one of many built during the State of Emergency. I had heard about these 'villages' as a teenager. Suspected Mau Mau sympathizers in the Kikuyu areas around Nairobi were rounded up, their huts burned to the ground, their homes confiscated by the Government, or their land transferred to Kikuyus loyal to the colonial government, fighting the Mau Mau. The men were sent into prisons and detention camps, some never to return, as in the case of Stephen's father. The Kikuyu women and children were herded into brutal barbed wire villages. Askaris controlled everyone from their lookout towers. One or more women with their children were allocated to each imprisoning hut. The village near our home may have included women and children taken away in raids of servants' quarters within the city limits at the time of 'Operation Anvil.'

Now I pass groups of these women daily, trudging uphill,

returning to that village. They are bent over with bound loads of *kuni* (firewood), supported by a leather strap over their foreheads. I know they have laboured all day in the hot sun, clearing scrub and weeds for a few measly shillings.

'Kenya's Independence has brought them nothing,' I think to myself, as I rattle past them in my empty VW Kombi. 'I'm sure they must recognise my faded tomato red van, with its distinct colourful map of many countries. It means nothing to them, except for the obvious fact that I'm driving a big empty vehicle.'

'*If only this Bwana would give us a lift*' they must be thinking.

Every day, the thought runs through my mind that at one time that could have been Steven's mother trudging up that exhausting hill.

One day I impulsively stop near the Westlands roundabout and offer a ride to a group of six women. Grateful, they place their bundles of kuni and their pangas, on the van floor and squat inside leaning against the sides of the van. I take them as far as my gate at the end of Peponi Road. This has cut at least six miles off their arduous daily trek home.

The next morning they are waiting at the top of my drive for a ride in the other direction towards town. Soon it becomes routine. Neither side misses a day.

It has gone on for months now. Most days they will chatter among themselves in their tribal Kikuyu. Sometimes, they will break into song; a happy catchy rhythmic chant that continues even after I drop them off. I ask Stephen to tell me what they're singing about.

"They are saying *Mungu Ngai* (God) has sent Stephen's *bapa* (father) to help them." Stephen struts proudly to the gate every morning, greeting them and wishing them a happy day and very often he's there to help them unload their kuni and pangas on the return journey.

* *

December 12, 1967 marks the fourth anniversary of Kenya's Uhuru. The stores in the Indian Bazaar on Biashara Street, Westlands, Lavington and Ngong Road, are stocked with imported seasonal goods targeted to appeal to Wageni customers. The prices are out of reach to Kenyans. New rumours surface of incipient corruption in some government departments. Work Permits, Business Licences, Tax-Clearance Certificates, among other mandatory documents are now available, targeted at non-African residents wishing to prolong their sojourn in this Garden of Eden.

* *

In December the air is crisp. Fresh layers of lavender-coloured petals cover the front patio; weaverbirds engage in hysterical chatter as they rest among the Jacaranda, and a fresh morning sun embraces our universe. Cloto comes out of his kennel for a big stretch and goes looking for Stephen. Eleanor joins me outside for a morning cuppa, before my 'matatu-hikers' arrive at the gate. It's their timetable that now seems to control my schedule.

"Alice and I are going to Plums Lane again today," she murmurs as Alice feeds comfortably at her breast.

"How come?"

"Well, your Mum is enjoying Alice so much, and I'm really fascinated by her stories. She's been filling me in on so many details of the family. For example: Did you know that she's still full of remorse over sending you to boarding school in Goa?"

"It wasn't her, it was Dad. He was convinced the Jesuits would trim my sails. I was too much of an independent thinker for him. According to his standards, I needed some good old fashioned Jesuit discipline instilled into me."

"Well… they did a good job, in my opinion. Thank you Jesuits! Oh, there are your dancing girls waiting for you," Eleanor points to 'the gang of six' and their pangas, at the top of the drive. Stephen and Cloto are keeping them occupied.

* *

That evening, Eleanor is bubbling over again with fresh news from Mum.

"Linda and Paul are coming to Nairobi for Christmas. Did you know that?" she asks.

"I know now," I reply. "It will be our Alice's first Christmas, so we must all make it special."

"Mum is making sure of that. She's already bought gifts for each of the six kids, to be presented by Father Christmas at the Goan Gymkhana Children's Party on December 23rd. So Lando, please make a note of that date."

"Wait. Six? How's that?"

"There's Linda's Paul; our Alice; Fatima's Lynette, Melanie and Vanessa; and your little brother, Frank."

"I'd forgotten about Frank. He's six-and-a-half so I suppose he's still eligible. I think the kid-gift cut-off age should be, ten."

"I doubt you'll feel that way about a cut-off date when Alice is ten." Eleanor chuckles.

* *

The Christmas of 1967 is very special, particularly for Mum and Dad. It will be the first time all the children and grandchildren will be together since Linda first left for the UK in 1961. Only Joachim will be missing. He's at Yale on a scholarship and not due back in Kenya for another six months. The excitement in the family is palpable.

The next day, Eleanor has more news. "Linda and Paul arrive on Thursday. Mum says you'll be going to the airport with Ahmad to pick them up. Look at this photo your mum gave me of her, Dad, and Linda taken at Christmas, 1936, thirty-one years ago, when Linda was the age of Alice."

"I haven't seen this one before. Dad is wearing his one posh suit that only comes out for weddings and funerals. I bet he'll wear it again for his retirement party from the National Bank of India next year."

* *

On Thursday, Ahmad and I meet Linda and Paul at JKIA. Paul was very excited to be driven in a Chevy. "We don't have such big cars in England," he shouted.

We go straight to Plums Lane where Mum, Eleanor, Fatima and all the babies are assembled to meet them. The menfolk are all at work and Niven is at school. Mum is very emotional and for a few moments speechless. She embraces Linda for a very long time – the loving embrace of a mother for her first born, irrespective of gender. A mother will never forget the experience of her first labour pains; the anxiety of responding to the twitches and turns of her own tiny flesh and blood and beating heart; the hours of constant watching and waiting; listening in the silence of the night for an uneven breath; a misplaced snore or snort…or for that matter, the surprise discovery of those first tiny baby farts.

I can see that Paul is restless. His uncle Frank does not hold any interest for him. Neither do any of his female cousins. He seems to remember me visiting his home with Eleanor. I offer my hand. He wraps his little fingers around it. Whiskey offers him a wet kiss and a wagging tail. Paul cautiously strokes the dog but clearly repels any further advances.

We walk to the back of the house to inspect Mum's chicken coop with the huge avocado tree standing tall in the centre. I sense Paul is intrigued but a little frightened. A few chickens rush towards us. Paul lets out a blood-curdling scream, and rushes to the safety of his mother.

He then drags Linda by the hand to come and scrutinize these strange birds that he has never seen before, not even at the Regents Park Zoo in London. She explains that they are chickens. An argument follows. "But Mummy, all the chickens in England arrive frozen, wrapped in plastic, and live in the refrigerator." He is adamant.

He almost convinces me, that there are no live chickens in England. I imagine he could contentedly spend the rest of his holiday, gripping the wire netting from the outside and intently studying these strange beings.

Mum on the other hand, has decided that this year she will re-enact the ritual of preparing traditional Goan Christmas sweets, called '*consuade*.' It was the way her generation, and the one before, transferred their cultural values from their native Goa to Kenya or anywhere Goans settled around the globe. Ethnicity, food, music, dance, arts and literature are the fundamental underpinnings of most cultures.

A *consuade* begins with the assembly of the basic ingredients. The wonderfully intoxicating aromas are provided by spices like: cinnamon, vanilla, cloves, cardamom, nutmeg, almonds, pistachios, ginger and saffron. A combination of these are roasted in turn, sending exotic fragrances throughout the house and wafting into the neighbourhood through open windows. Distinctive whiffs of roasted nuts, poppy seeds, sesame seeds mix with those of marinated dried fruit and in some cases spirits like rum, brandy and liqueurs.

Everything goes well. I hear Mum tell Linda how happy she is to have her back and helping in the kitchen again. "It is just like old times when you were a little girl."

She also confesses to Linda that she is very fond of Eleanor. "Lando chose well…she's not 'mean-spirited' like some of the European ladies who used to come to me to have their second-hand dresses altered. You should have heard how they gossiped about each other."

* *

Friday, December 22nd.

The complex preparations of the consuade, which peaked earlier that week, are over. Small trays laden with an assortment of sweets have been fashioned, and distributed to friends and neighbours. Other trays have been received in return. Many non-Goan neighbours bring flowers and chocolates.

Eleanor was at my mum's announcing that she would return home after lunch.

* *

While Eleanor and Alice are out, Stephen and I use the opportunity to walk the periphery of our plot of land and dream about future plans for the property.

As we reach the bottom of the incline, he discloses the fact that he's noticed an increase in the number of snakes down by the stream.

"I didn't want to say this in front of Miss Eranol, Bwana, but I think she does not like snakes."

"Well, Stephen, you are very observant. She loves almost every creature on earth but truly despises snakes. So it's good that you didn't bring it up.

"I think we can resolve the problem by building a retaining wall by the stream to keep them from migrating to our yard. They can bask in the sun to their hearts content without Eleanor ever having to meet their family," I muse with a smile.

I explain my hope and plan to one day, expand the main house, and convert his quarters into a proper guest cottage. Servant's quarters will not have a place in an independent Kenya. I'm sketching broad strokes for what I have in mind.

"Around the edges, we will plant two rows of Jacaranda, like this one," I point to one of our two magnificent trees. "The land in-between will have fruit trees; at least one of each variety: avocado, papaya, peach, apple, pear and guava." Stephen listens attentively then interjects…

"…What about pineapple, Bwana? Or mingi (many) bananas by the river," he chuckles, taking it as a joke since he understands that we don't have the money for such dreams… yet.

Cloto begins to bark before we even hear or see the Beetle coming down the driveway. We rush to meet Eleanor and Alice.

She carefully picks up the carrycot with our sleeping angel to take her indoors.

"Let's have a cuppa out here," she says. "I have a little surprise for you."

While I boil the kettle for tea, Eleanor shows me the surprise which is our share of Mum's traditional sweets. I test her to see if Mum's cultural infusion has worked, especially as the sweets have *Konkani* and Portuguese names. As she sets them out on a plate, I point to each one and she answers.

"*Bebinca, bolinas, kulkuls, cocada, neuros, bathica…*" She knows her stuff. I give her a hug and carry the tea tray with the sweets outside.

It's the first time after a very long period that we have actually been able to relax together. She says that she feels we have already lived a lifetime's worth, but it's not even a year since she first set foot in Africa. Eleanor confirms that

Alice's arrival has changed her life in so many ways…and so has Kenya. "If only there wasn't this constant worry about security and the growing rumours about corruption setting in, I could live here forever among the jacaranda!" She lets out a sigh as she looks up at our ceiling of blue and violet petals.

I pick up my sketchbook from the patio table. I show her my outline sketches for our dream home, with its open patios built like steps down the hillside. We talk about the landscaping… the fruit trees and the embrace of the jacaranda grove that would cushion us from the outside world.

"I too dream we may be able to bring up our children here, among the jacaranda."

* *

Saturday, December, 23rd

The Children's Christmas Party goes well. I did remember to write it into my schedule and we made it there with Alice on time.

It's a novelty for Paul who is a bit reluctant at first, but Frank and Lynette dive in and have themselves a rollicking good time. The rest of the children are too young, but Mum is ecstatically happy as she introduces anyone in close proximity, to her grandchildren. "Meet my wonderful little angels," she boasts.

* *

Christmas Eve, 1967

Mum helps Linda make some final adjustments to her dress. "Just like the old days," Mum says, "Your friends are going to be so happy to see you back in Nairobi again."

Eleanor and I are at Plums Lane around 4 PM when a car pulls in and parks in the driveway. A family of six roll out. The father was a classmate of my mother's in high school in Loutolim, Goa, in 1931. My mum and dad had remained friends with them ever since they arrived in Kenya. I had seen him a week earlier at City Hall, and took notice of his full head of grey hair which has now been dyed jet black. His wife is younger and all dolled up for the occasion. Their kids range from twelve down to two years of age.

Over tea and Christmas sweets, they announce that they won't be able to attend any of the planned social events. They have received their Canadian Landed Immigrant forms and will be flying to Toronto on Boxing Day. They'll need the next day to prepare. They have come to offer a final farewell and to thank Mum and Dad for being the first to welcome them to Africa with open arms in 1951, and for remaining such good friends. "I'm afraid you will not see us again," he says to Mum and Dad. I see their eyes well up.

Eleanor and I politely excuse ourselves, as we need to get the baby home to sleep. In the car, we talk about the sadness of watching families leave Africa to start afresh somewhere else in the world.

"You know they're only doing it to give the next generation a better future," Eleanor says, "just as we may have to do one day."

26

Christmas Day, 1967

After High Mass at St Francis Xavier Church, Parklands, we are back at Plums Lane for a light breakfast, and then the opening of more gifts for the children. Frank, Paul, Lynette and Melanie go outside to play. Vanessa and Alice are having a nap in an adjacent bedroom. The adults exchange random thoughts and memories of absent family members.

Dad had heard from Joachim in America. "Flying out for Christmas was out of the question. Joachim will meet Linda and Paul on his return trip via London next May."

Fatima remembers her late father-in-law who passed away in Goa on May 20th, just about a month before little Vanessa was born. Luiz speaks emotionally and with pride about his father, Dr. Francisco Antonio Vicente Gomes who was a famous Dental Surgeon and philanthropist in the Indian city of Poona. Luiz describes how his father had shaped his life and imbued in him his fundamental values and a strong sense of self-discipline. "It is these qualities that have enabled me to rise in my career."

Luiz was recently appointed to a top management position at the Queensway branch of the Barclay Bank, making us all proud.

"So many of our friends have been dying recently," Mum says, "Mrs. Pinto…"

"… Oh, gosh, look at the time," Fatima swiftly interjects in an effort to keep the conversation from becoming morose. "Come Mum I'll help you put the finishing touches to lunch while the men finish laying the table." With that Fatima nods to the men as she quickly escorts her mother from the dining room.

Dad winks at Luiz. That's code for them to surreptitiously migrate out of range. They adjourn to the front patio (veranda) and share a pre-lunch drink. Niven and I are the only able-bodied 'men' still standing, so we get down to work. At Plums Lane, the formal adult dining table is in the enclosed rear veranda. There is also a smaller table set up separately for the kids.

Linda emerges from a bedroom with two large boxes of colourful Christmas Crackers from England. "These are the real thing; not those cheap imitations from Japan they sell in the Westlands' stores. Those barely make a sound when they pop."

We place a festive cracker by each place setting. Eleanor returns from the garden with a clutch of glorious Christmas-red hibiscus blooms. She lays them carefully along the length of the table with studied casualness for a final artistic touch. Eleanor, Niven and I step back to admire the beautiful table setting. Everything is festive and colourful. "Damn," Niven says, "I forgot my camera at the dorm at Strathmore."

Mum pokes her head out of the kitchen. "One of you please herd everyone to the table. We will serve in fifteen minutes. Niven, please make sure all the children have washed their hands before they come to the table."

Mum had told Eleanor, "it will be a 'traditional' Christmas lunch," but she had a surprise for her new daughter-in-law. Earlier that morning a Goan man delivered a large neatly wrapped package with an outer layer of Christmas wrapping and tinsel. Mum had called me into the kitchen to help unwrap the parcel. She had decided to delight Eleanor with a traditional Goan roasted suckling pig. To keep the secret, she placed the order with a family who lived in Ruaraka, off the Thika Road. One of their enterprises was catering for private Goan events that required traditional dishes from the motherland. A greeting card was attached to the parcel, thanking Mum for the order. Inside was a neatly written note: *'Since the number of Goans is declining rapidly in Kenya, our family has decided to close the business and move to Portugal in the New Year…'*

Besides the suckling pig, other dishes include a variety of typical vegetable dishes, steamed rice and a 'pukka' Goan prawn and okra coconut curry with an abundant helping of pickles and relishes. I catch Eleanor's eye across the table and she offers me a cheeky nod toward the splendid Goan/Indian banquet. I grin in response as I recall her first attempt to impress me with her version of Indian cuisine. I conclude the incident would be best left unmentioned today in the light of this incredible feast.

We all raise a toast to Mum for a superb spread. Dad makes a short speech welcoming Linda and Paul. He welcomes Eleanor again into the family, and raises a toast to her parents and her brother. "And a special toast to Linda's David in the UK," he adds.

There is a choice for dessert, but there are few takers as everyone has literally 'pigged out.' Succulent bits still cling to the bones of the roast but it has been reduced to the head and skeleton.

With tummies full, the children dash off outdoors to continue the interrupted war games. The adults urge Mum to take a break. "Please, sit back and relax Mum, we'll clear the dirty dishes," I insist.

"But for now everyone, let's just pile them in the sink and on the counter."

Mum suggests Dad follow the tradition they had evolved over the years, so we are all shooed like a herd of Maasai cattle into the living room. Dad sits at the piano, rolls up his sleeves and launches, with unrestrained gusto, into a medley of tunes; 'White Christmas', 'Jingle Bells', 'Ramona', 'We'll Meet Again,' 'La Paloma.'

Linda leans over and whispers to him that she regrets giving up her music lessons. She was the only one in our family who completed all her music grades at the Catholic Parochial School. She still remembers being rapped on the knuckles with a ruler. Those nuns were really strict.

There's a short lull in the music, while Dad tries to recall some of his other favourite tunes. Eleanor stands up. I notice that her wine glass is empty. Her face is flushed but she smiles and begins to speak, which takes me by surprise.

"I'm normally shy …I know that for a fact…but I must share a lovely story that Mum told me recently. It's about Dad." Mum sits up and pays attention.

"Mum told me that ever since Linda passed her driving test more than ten years ago, she realised how much married Goan women were missing. They were totally dependent on their menfolk for income and stability, but it was their mobility being hindered that truly bothered her. Even to shop for basic food and household items, a wife had to travel on buses, or catch a taxi, or on special occasions, rely on friends. Mum finally determined that she was going to learn to drive. And that she would have a car by Christmas of 1967. Dad was not convinced it was necessary or even possible.

"So this past February, she quietly began to take private lessons. She paid the trainer in cash from her little savings stash. She practised at the club on weekday mornings when the members were at work. Dad heard about it from one of the Club's grounds maintenance men but he pretended he didn't know.

"Then this past April, on her 50th birthday, Dad sent Ahmad in his cab, to bring her into town. He took her directly into the showroom of Hughes Motors on Kenyatta Avenue and presented her with the brand new green Ford Anglia, which she now drives everywhere. It was titled and insured in her name, ready to drive out. She had achieved what she wanted.

"I had to tell this story as it will be an inspiration for the next generation that seems to be made up predominately of girls. Congratulations Mum and Dad."

Mum stands up to the thunderous applause. Her eyes are moist. She gives Dad a peck on his forehead, then walks over to Eleanor and hugs her.

"Thank you, all of you. Now you had all better rest, otherwise you will be too tired to dance tonight." She exits to her bedroom. With misty eyes, Dad follows her.

Fatima and Luiz collect their brood and head home. They will not be going to the Christmas Dance tonight as they have invited the whole family for a Boxing Day lunch at their Westlands home and they need time to prepare. Eleanor and I are staying overnight with the baby, but we're going to the dance and Niven is the appointed baby sitter.

* *

Mum, Dad, Linda, Eleanor and I arrive at the Club at about 8:30 P.M. Our ladies are beautifully attired and the men are not too shabby either.

Linda prefers the grander New Year's Eve dance, but the Christmas Day dance is Mum's favourite social of all. Mum has always loved dancing and Dad doesn't mind her dancing with another partner… in fact, he loves it because it lets him off the hook. Now that his knees are beginning to grumble he prefers to sit with his buddies and talk over old times.

As always, the hall is beautifully decorated. Balloons, tinsel, streamers, special sparkling lights abound. The last of the better known Goan bands in Nairobi is playing. The

Christmas Dance has by tradition been open only to members, their families and any out-of-town family and friends. Other Goan clubs have similar restrictions. It is meant to create a more intimate evening where members who have grown up and shared in the community can greet each other and catch up on news. This year we know almost everyone will be talking about the declining membership and their families spreading across the globe like seeds scattered in the wind.

But there is elation and even some surprise, in meeting friends who haven't yet left, or have decided to stay in Kenya. The musicians ensure that the music is joyous and lively. The Emcee has planned the playlist well. The evening will have many prize-dances. The winners will be selected by elimination dances like *musical chairs* but without the chairs.

During an elimination dance, Linda sees Mum slump onto her partner's shoulder. She runs to Eleanor and I on the dance floor. She grabs my arm and pulls me toward Mum. Her dance partner is calling for help. Three men rush over and carry her to a chair. Her head is now slumped to one side. Above the din of the music, the Emcee makes an urgent call for a doctor over the P.A.

Dr. Manu D'Cruz, a renowned E.N.T Specialist is close by. He takes charge. An ambulance is immediately called. Within seconds there are three more doctors by Mum's side: Dr. Maisie Fernandes, Dr. Albert Da Costa, and Dr. Arnold Carvalho. A message is relayed from a lookout at the other end of the hall. 'The ambulance has arrived!'

I overhear a doctor tell Linda that Mum has quite possibly

had a brain hemorrhage. Linda insists on riding in the ambulance with her and I'm pleased, as Linda is a highly qualified nurse, trained in London.

"Where's Dad?" I ask. I am directed to him. He is seated. Pale. He has shock written over his face. Frightened eyes. His hands are trembling.

He needs to go home and rest or I fear, he too might end up in hospital tonight. I signal Eleanor to come with me. I take her and Dad back to Plums Lane. She will stay with him, Alice and the boys, while I drive to Fatima and Luiz's house to let them know what has happened. They rush immediately to the hospital. I will stay behind to babysit their daughters, until they return. Then I will go and sit in the waiting room with Linda.

They return about two hours later and I know from their faces that it's over for my beloved Mum. She has left us at fifty years and eight months.

At the hospital, Linda tells me that she knew in the ambulance that it was a massive attack. Mum's pulse had dropped very low and was barely discernable. She slid into a coma and her breathing had become laborious. "By the time we arrived at the hospital, which took barely five minutes, the doctor was shaking his head indicating there was little hope of recovery."

Ninety minutes later, I drive Linda to Plums Lane. The house is quiet and dark. I turn on a table lamp and see Dad slumped in a chair. We rush to him. His eyes flutter but he is breathing. He says he's okay but wishes to remain where he is.

All around there is evidence of the joy and laughter we

shared only a few hours earlier. Children's toys are strewn about; wrapping paper shoved under the sofa to get it out of the way.

Eleanor suddenly appears in a white dressing gown like a friendly ghost emerging from the shadows. She has been sobbing all night. Her eyes are swollen. We hold each other close. She isn't quite sure what to do.

"Let me make you and Linda some coffee," she whispers.

"Let me do it, Luv. You stay here with Dad and Linda. Would you prefer *Ovaltine* in warm milk?" I ask. Eleanor offers a wan smile. I know her preference.

"Coffee for me please," Linda says. I nod and set off on my mission.

The kitchen scene is a horror. Dishes are piled high in the sink and on the countertops. Stuffed or not, Niven and the others were clearly foraging for food, after we left for the dance. They had attacked what was left of the suckling pig. The bones were scraped clean; but they left the head strategically facing the doorway in the hope that it would freak out the first person to enter the kitchen.

I drape a tea towel over it. I'm not in the mood for childish pranks tonight.

The mess will have to wait. I know our lives are about to undergo an upheaval. According to Goan tradition, there will be a constant stream of visitors who will come to the house to pay their respects. At best we might hope for a day's peace before the people begin to arrive. Fortunately Dad agrees to go to his bed.

We barely have a couple of hours before the boys will be up and curious. When they do rise, Linda breaks the news gently. Over the next few days, everything we expected, and others we did not, happens.

Mum was much loved by neighbours who came bearing gifts of food. Stephen brings his mother and sister from their village. Mary (ayah) comes too. The gardeners from the nearby Plums Hotel come around to say *'pole'* (sorry); three ladies from the Parklands Sports Club who became friends with her after she did their alterations arrive, and of course there are streams of Goans. There are friends from Kericho, Kisumu and Nakuru.

During this terrible time, the strike by employees of Nairobi City Council goes into a second week and to make a difficult situation impossible, the gravediggers at the Langata Cemetery join the strike the day after mum's passing. All burials are postponed indefinitely.

Fortunately the strike was short-lived and two days later Mum was buried with all of us present to honour her. It was the most painful trauma we'd ever suffered as a family. Linda will stay on to help Dad out for another few days and Fatima, Luiz, Eleanor and I will continue to visit Dad regularly.

But the truth is… nothing will ever be the same again at Plums Lane.

* *

It's January 5th, our first wedding anniversary. I'm arriving home in the late afternoon somewhat exhausted. Eleanor was asleep when I left the house this morning. The sun filters its warm light through the delicate petals of the jacaranda. Eleanor is fast asleep on the patio. I give her a gentle kiss on the lips. "Happy Anniversary Sweetheart."

"Oh thank you, Luv," she smiles. "I guess I dozed off. I'm so tired. I can't believe what we've been through in only one year," She gestures me to keep my voice low as Alice is asleep in her carrycot under a mosquito net.

"Lando my darling, what will happen to us now?"

"The next fifty are bound to be better," I reply in as reassuring a voice as I can muster. Of course I have no idea.

"Fatima called about an hour ago. She told me that Niven left yesterday for Strathmore to continue his residency. So now, it's just going to be Dad and Frank at home together. She's worried about what will happen now."

"Why? What about?"

"She said Dad called her. He sounded very angry. He said Frank doesn't listen to him anymore, and keeps disappearing from the house."

"I suppose I'd better go and check on them now. Do you mind if we postpone our anniversary dinner tonight, Luv? Just don't feel like it in the circumstances."

"You took the words out of my mouth darling. I have already cooked a modest dinner, and have told Mary we will not be requiring her babysitting tonight."

I quickly freshen up and head to Plums Lane. Peponi Road is congested with rush-hour traffic, especially near the Westlands roundabout.

Whiskey greets me with great exuberance. He must be

missing Mum terribly. It is quiet. There is no sign of Frank. I find Dad sitting in his rocking chair looking extremely upset.

"Hello Dad!"

When he sees it's me he shouts angrily. "Where's Frank? Have you seen Frank?"

"Sorry, Dad, I haven't. Did he say where he was going?" I ask.

"No. That boy has completely stopped listening to me. Please go find him," he begs.

"I'll go, Dad," I say. "Come Whiskey, let's go find Frank."

"I venture out into the garden. Whiskey is excited to be running around again but I can tell he's missing Mum's tender care. I call out… "Frank! Frank! Where are you?" There is no reply.

"Come Whiskey, let's try out there." I shout as I walked toward the gate and Plums Lane. Whiskey begins to bark excitedly and runs towards a patch of corn planted on public land. I follow him. I see a slight movement among the corn stalks. I walk lightly towards it.

There, sitting among the tall stalks, silently weeping, is Frank. He looks up at me with tears and terror in his eyes. I embrace him and help him to his feet. "Come inside now Frank. Dad is worried about you."

It is already dark as I make my way back to Eleanor on the dimly-lit and winding Peponi Road. There are voices reverberating inside my head… "Lando…Lando, what will happen to us now?"

- End -

The Photograph (c. 1937) given by Mum to Eleanor (1967)

Photo taken in the rear garden of neighbour Mr. Olivet Almeida (PWD). Ten years later as recounted in 'Beyond The Cape' Lando releases the handbrake and lets the car roll down the slope at Lando's home, with a loadful of happy kids. He had only a normal ten-year-old brain. He ran into an electric pole to slow the car down. It caused a power outage in whole neighbourhood. Spanking, curfew for a week, Confession and penance followed. The Almeidas refused to visit ever again. Lando believed this incident was the proverbial straw that broke the camel's back. He was sent to a Jesuit run boarding school in Goa, until his big escape two years later.

Author's Note

A Primer: Goans of British East Africa

Sometime in the future, African historians will tell about a tribe of brown men and women to came to their land of East Africa, stayed for a while and then joined an exodus in the mid-sixties to seek new opportunities elsewhere. They left behind a legacy in many spheres of human endeavor.

In Africa, the arrival of Europeans in the 1500s (almost simultaneously with their arrival in Goa) led to the colonization of vast tracts of coastal land, and to the near annihilation of indigenous people and cultures. Newly acquired territories in the 'New World' required labour. Enslaved Africans became 'black gold' for the white man, and were forced onto slave ships. The Portuguese took the first slaves to Brazil as early as 1575. Various estimates put the total number between three million and four million.

By the mid-eighteenth century, Africa was like a large pie surrounded by ants nibbling at its edges. The west coast was dotted with slave-trading centres often backed by small fortresses and ports for other merchandise. The east coast trading ports served Arab and Persian slave traders and Indian merchants of Asia-bound trade.

In the nineteenth century, with the discovery of larger and more varied mineral deposits, the pace of colonization grew, with European countries rushing to claim more territory. The Berlin Conference was hosted by Germany in 1884, bringing fourteen (14) European countries together in an attempt to bring order to the land scramble. Turkey and the United States were invited as observers. No African kingdoms or countries were represented.

About ninety days later, Africa, with a land mass of approximately 11.61 million square miles (almost three times the size of the United States) had been divided into fifty (50) territories, parcelled out to seven (7) European colonial powers, of which Britain was a major player. The boundaries were arbitrary and did not respect ethnic or cultural definitions, in part resulting for much of today's inter-territorial conflicts. Each of the seven countries now embarked on a race to colonize its African 'possessions'.

Britain, having successfully stopped the slave trade in its territories, resorted to indentured labour, in which workers were contracted for a fee and predetermined period, to support colonization. For just such a purpose, Britain took thousands of Indians to East Africa to build the Kenya-Uganda railway in the 1890s. Many stayed behind at the end of their contracts.

By the twentieth century, British rulers were desperate to colonize East Africa with its own settlers. They also needed administrators and accountants, bartenders and bakers, cooks and clerks, musicians and mechanics, engineers and tailors, doctors, and even domestics. They turned to Goa (then a Portuguese colony) for these.

The people of Goa suited the bill perfectly, as they created no *matata* ('trouble' in Swahili), spoke English, wore Western attire, and drank Scotch whisky. They played card games and cricket. Although they gyrated to the *mando* and *dulpod*, they also danced the lancer, the waltz, and the foxtrot. They were Catholic and considered reliable to handle the public purse strings. Loyal to the point of being docile, they did what they were told. Above all, compared to the cost of British labour, they could be had cheaper—very much cheaper indeed. They flocked to East Africa.

The first generation of Goan immigrants struggled against many adverse aspects of colonial life, especially economic exclusion and racial segregation. But they carried their capacity for social interaction and adaptability with them. They built social clubs. They funded their own Catholic schools - brown Catholics were not admitted into schools for white Catholics. They sacrificed, as parents do, to ensure that their children would have a better life.

By the early 60s, Britain had exited from its colonies. The Goan second generation (my generation) were in their twenties and late teens. They emigrated alone, or accompanied families to new pastures in faraway lands in the UK, Canada, Australia, USA, Portugal, Brazil, among others. Some moved back to retire in their ancestral home in Goa, since 1961 a state in the Indian Union. That was before the arrival of the *Internet and Google*. Most did not know what to expect. They became bogged down immediately dealing with immigration and economic issues of their own. Some stayed behind and dreamed that life would be different after colonialism. The achievements of those who left and those that opted to remain, and their personal stories were never told, until new Goan writers started to emerge.

A full list of Goan authors and reviews will be founded at website:
http://britishempire.co.uk/library/beyondthecape.htm

To quote Mr. Luscombe:
"The Goan community found an unlikely niche within the British Empire despite being from a Portuguese colony dating back some four centuries and having undergone a completely different imperial experience to most people from the Indian sub-continent. The Portuguese Empire had been around longer than the British one and its colonies stretched back towards Africa and on to Europe via Mozambique, Angola and Brazil amongst other colonies. Many Goans had also embraced Catholicism over these intervening centuries - although as this book makes clear in a defiantly Goan manner. The combination of Christianity, a industrious work ethic and strong familial and commercial links across the Portuguese Empire meant that Goans were more at ease than most Indians in crossing the Indian ocean in search of new opportunities whilst still keeping fierce links to their land of their birth and their distinctive Goan culture."

Acknowledgements

First, I wish to thank especially Mr. Stephen Luscombe, scholar, teacher, world traveller and curator of the website (britishempire.co.uk) for his reviews of my two earlier books. These gave me the confidence to continue writing in spite of some unforeseen challenges, and reinforced the relevance my MATATA SERIES books. http://britishempire.co.uk/library/beyondthecape.htm

I am deeply indebted to a number of people who helped jog my memory on past events to bring *Among the Jacaranda-Buds of Matata in Kenya*, to fruition. Some persons are named in this novel (although others wished to participate as fictional characters): Aquinas De Souza, Betsy and Ritchie Pinto, Blanche and Luiz Gomes, Catherine Marston, David and Flora Mutiso, Edward Marston, Nigel Moor, Sarita Menezes, and Sylvia DeMello for specific contributions.

My regular cheerleaders: Ann Barns and Sasha Menezes, for reading innumerable drafts, making suggestions, and helping to refine the story.

I could not turn this manuscript into a book without my professional team: My Editor Reva Leah Stern and Rudi Rodrigues, CEO, Avatar Inc. Toronto for (Cover and Art Direction, Interior Book Design). However none of the above named must be held responsible for any of my shortcomings.

During long periods of solitary confinement, it was my partner, Norma Starkie, who supplied me with food rations and water - a thankless task! And finally thank you my readers. Your comments will always be welcome.

Braz Menezes, Burlington, ON, Canada
http://matatabooks.com/htp

About The Author

Braz Menezes is a Commonwealth Scholar who studied Creative Writing at George Brown College and attended the mentorship program at Humber College in Toronto. His work has previously appeared in various anthologies including Canadian Voices, Volumes 1&2&3; Goa Masala; Indian Voices; and Canadian Imprints. His debut novel *Just Matata: Sin, Saints and Settlers* (2011) was expanded and issued as a Second Edition titled *Beyond the Cape – Sin, Saints, Slaves, and Settlers* (2015). Book Two of the Matata Trilogy titled *More Matata: Love after the Mau Mau* first came out in 2012.

Among the Jacaranda – Buds of Matata in Kenya is planned for release in August 2018. The author is currently working on a fourth Matata book.

Braz Menezes was born in British-ruled Kenya to parents from Goa, India (then Portuguese India). He decided to chronicle his experience of living through the last fifty years of Imperial power in the Portuguese and British Empires, in the Matata Series. (*Matata* means trouble in Kiswahili).

He has travelled extensively in Brazil, Mexico, Egypt, India, Pakistan, Sri Lanka, and South Korea, among others, with the World Bank. Before this he led a different life as an architect and urban planner. He turned to the pen to escape retirement and now lives in Burlington, Ontario, Canada.

Excerpts from Readers

Comments on earlier books (Matata Series)

It is just good, old-fashioned story-telling at its best...a beautifully nuanced account that holds your attention and interest.

I would hate for someone not to read this book as they thought that it might be too specific an account of just one community in one part of the Empire. Nothing could be further from the truth.

Issues of hierarchy, race, religion, morality all find themselves worked into the wider themes of family, community, education, economic opportunities and bureaucratic realities all within the wider imperial framework.

Hats off to Braz Menezes for not shying away from difficult issues and addressing them in a highly believable and informative manner.

Once again, the author manages to continue to weave the compelling story of the Goan community through the very last years of imperial British rule and takes Lando's story through to the new dawn of an independent Kenya...I look forward to reading how Lando's dreams, aspirations, hopes and fears all unfold in a post-colonial world.

Stephen Luscombe UK
https://www.britishempire.co.uk/library/beyondthecape.htm

You are really a good storyteller. You have the makings of a good novelist. You have a feel for the land and the people (as individuals and as part of groups- ethnicities, castes). You are able to sum up history and the way it figures in the present in a very interesting way in a few pages (e.g. what is said about caste).

Several episodes are very dramatic. The chapters are short, almost anecdotal. There is a fine sense of humour and irony in the chapter titles. I am impressed at how much you know, and how much I learned from the novel.

Peter Nazareth USA, Professor of English,
Advisor to International Program, U.IOWA

What makes the historical novels of author Braz Menezes so fascinating is his lively and exciting narrative style, which entices the reader to follow him wherever he guides, lures, and leads you, often with a very delightful sense of self-deprecating humour.

The narrative is so compelling, you cannot help but identify with Lando and his varied matata plight, both real or imagined. In fact, the reader is virtually transformed in becoming Lando, and living his life with him and for him.
Gerhard Fuerst, USA, Former Adjunct Professor, Michigan State University

The unhitching of a country from its colonial presence always makes interesting reading... When lived by the settler-people of that day, it is always traumatic. To narrate this without seeking sympathy or victimhood is creditable. When told matter-of-factly, it makes for a good book.
Roland Francis, CA

The book, always interesting and - thanks goodness - not conventional, proved to be a real page-turner. I loved it, not least the author's quiet sense of humour. I am greatly looking forward to the sequel.
Michael Hanka, UK

I could not put this book down until the very last page.
A great book. Mr. Menezes writes about the life and times of a young man growing up and living in Kenya under British Colonial rule, the racial tensions it brought about but it is also about a love and romance that follows, makes compelling reading.
D. Pimenta, UK

A book I just couldn't put down and which I feel those of us who were once "WaGoa wa Kenya" will thoroughly enjoy.
Mervyn Maciel, Author, Bwana Karani and From Toto to Mzee

Menezes also engages with all five of the senses when he is writing and the combined effect by the end of a chapter, let alone the end of the book, is vividly intense.
Aamera Jiwaji, Kenya, writing in AwaaZ Magazine

I was going to hold on until I started my holiday, but I couldn't resist opening the first page, and then the next and the next, until I've done one chapter already. I am completely captivated. I love your book and I think I'm going to get through it before I even start my vacation.
Joan Do Rosario, CA

I find that I telephone my children and tell them stories of my life as a child, and when they receive their copies of 'Just Matata' shortly I think they will begin to understand why my memories are coming back...So thank you for this journey I am making as I read your book.

Luisa Heaton, UK

A beautifully written book where the author manages to capture the reader's imagination right from the start – I found it difficult to put it down – and when I finished reading the book, I ruminated on many sections of the book for some time afterwards.

This book, again, demonstrates the author's incredible skills in telling a story through the use of appropriate words and language so that the reader 'sees' – and feels - the author's own experiences, with quite a few entertaining experiences (as seen through the eyes of an 11-year old boy) interspersed throughout the book. Of note, in particular, is how the author's emotions are so easily transferred to the reader – an exceptional skill. I now have nothing to go on to until the author releases his third book!

Sylvia DeMello, Educator

I absolutely loved these books, which are well written and fast moving. Having been born and raised in Kenya myself, Braz's books were especially interesting to me for their insight into what life was like in this most beautiful and wonderful African country. However, not everything on the surface was as it seemed, for it hid a darker side during Colonial times, and Braz has really brought this to light; the struggle for independence, the difficulties faced by non-white Kenyans as the colour bar was enforced, and most painful the horrors of the Mau Mau. Being in the thick of these times as a school boy and young University student to his first love and exciting career working on Kenya's first wildlife tourist lodges, Braz's hero Lando is a insight into the life of a young Goan man during that period.

Rosalind Wallqvist, Sweden

Notes

Notes

Made in the USA
Columbia, SC
13 August 2018